MARC MOSS-JONES AND KEVIN CORE

I Don't Like Your Tie

100 takes on the joke that made The Beatles

First edition

This book was professionally typeset on Reedsy. Find out more at reedsy.com

Foreword

The Beatles showed very little evidence of understanding Planck's Constant or second-order phase transitions, and produced no peer-reviewed work. Why then am I, a Professor of Theoretical Physics, writing the foreword to a book about them?

I am in fact well-qualified for the task. Firstly, in my youth, I played briefly in a group as part of the nascent 'Merseybeat' scene. Secondly, I own eleven ties.

My quartet shared a bill with The Beatles on a number of occasions. I found them to be affable, if over-familiar. While George Harrison did not comment upon anyone's neckwear, on 2nd March 1962 in the dressing room of St John's Hall Bootle he did say to me: 'I don't like your thigh.'

During this period I saw scant indication of the success they were later to enjoy. Indeed, any impartial observer may have found it difficult to see why they, rather than any another band performing on such nights, won worldwide acclaim.

I believe, just as in the formation of the universe, chance plays a role.

I abandoned music and have found my sixty years in Theoretical Physics to be reasonably fulfilling. It would be completely inaccurate to suggest I missed standing behind the curtain before the buzz of an excited crowd, the memorable hum of a Vox AC30 amplifier, or the illusory camaraderie of being in a 'band'. Plus, given that all music is in essence soundwaves and the displacement of air, my songs *from a scientific perspective* were every bit as 'good' as theirs.

These experiences in no way shaped my research focus on the pivotal exchange between Georges Martin and Harrison on 6th June 1962, and quest to isolate the theoretical fulcrum of exponential Beatlism, more properly referred to as the 'Neck Event Horizon'. Less relevant still is my December 1974 particle accelerator experiment which considered time dilation in muons in relation to said Neck Event Horizon. The accelerator's successful targeting of that moment gave me some confidence in the possibility of fracturing the 'Fab Alpha' timeline.

I had long posited that the various resulting timelines might coalesce at a quantum level in the minds of subjects sufficiently obsessed with The Beatles. I congratulate Messrs Moss-Jones and Core on their collation of these data, and on their book, which has been competently typeset and bound.

In closing, I would like to make the point that The Tommy Parbold Four did NOT perform Long Tall Sally at the end of our set in Lathom Hall on 3rd August 1961 in order to 'spoil' the ending to The Beatles own closing set, as has been alleged in some books. The choice was, and remains, a coincidence.

Professor T Parbold

Planck Chair in Theoretical Physics, Norwegian University of Science and Technology

[1]

GEORGE MARTIN: Then George piped up: 'I don't like your tie.' We all had a good laugh at that, I must say. Then he turned round to look at Pete and said 'I don't like your tie'. Then he looked at Paul and said 'I don't like your tie'. We'd stopped laughing by this point. Then he looked at John and said 'I don't like your tie'. Then he pointed at Norman Smith and said 'I don't like your tie'. Then he pointed at Ron Richards and said 'I don't like your tie'. Then he pointed at Chris Neal and said 'I don't like your tie'. Then he pointed at Ken Townsend and said 'I don't like your tie'. Then he pointed at Brian Epstein and said 'I don't like your tie'. Then he looked at the tape machine and said 'I don't like your tie'. None of us knew what to do. He was still saying it as they carried him out. I never saw him again.

[2]

GEORGE MARTIN: 'Yeah' George said 'I don't like your tie.'

I looked back at him, a little surprised. 'You're not suggesting I take it off, surely?' I said with a smile. They all fell about at this. I usually wore a slightly wider tie to work in those days, not quite those kipper things we had in the seventies, but wide enough to cover my modesty.

I remember looking at John; he had a big pimple on his thigh, almost a boil actually, and Paul next to him, both of them surprisingly hairless in the chest area.

One of them, John I think, made as if to take his own tie off there and then. We all laughed – typical John, as I later found out. He even actually swung it to one side and gave us all a flash of his private area.

George grinned and went to the other extreme, fanning out the two ends of his tie to give himself more coverage. Pete was right at the back, head down, saying nothing. I could just see his hairy leg poking out from the end of the mixing console.

There's not much more to tell about that occasion really, I just remember shaking each of them by the hand as they left, and watching as this line of eight buttocks disappeared off down the corridor.

I had no idea the owners of those buttocks would change the world.

[3]

GEORGE MARTIN: Then George piped up in that slow, rather deliberate voice of his. 'Yeah, I don't like your tie'.

I didn't know what to say. George wasn't to know but that tie was actually a present from my then-secretary Judy, who went on of course to become my wife. It seems silly now, but that remark really upset me. I probably shouldn't have taken it so personally but when you don't really know someone the smallest thing can affect your whole view of them.

The silence was becoming a little awkward so I covered my hurt with a laugh. They joined in and we passed the remainder of the session pretty amicably. But inside just I couldn't get past what he'd said. I'm afraid from that point I could never shake off the feeling that The Beatles were laughing at me.

We did some great work together as everyone knows, but we never really gelled and I ended up spending more and more time on my other acts. I don't think we worked together after about late 1964. Then Parlophone dropped them, they moved over to Pye and things went downhill for them, rather. They split in... '65 was it?

[4]

NORMAN SMITH: George Harrison looked at George Martin and said 'Yeah, I don't like your tie!' There was a pause, then Martin *launched* himself at Harrison. I'd never seen anything like it. He got hold of Harrison's hair and pulled his head so he was inches from Harrison's face. 'What did you say?' he snarled. Harrison wriggled free and punched Martin in the head. It wasn't a hard blow but it knocked him off balance, enough for Lennon to come in with a kick to the stomach. Martin let out an inhuman roar and grabbed Harrison by the throat. By this point McCartney and Best had lashed three mic stands together with a length of quarter-inch tape and came at Martin, using it as a kind of battering ram - caught him right in the base of his spine. He howled and turned to face them, letting go of Harrison. Martin grabbed the weapon and launched it at McCartney. You'll note Paul walks with a slight limp to this day.

Then quick as a flash Martin's kneeling on Harrison's chest, taking his own tie off. 'Don't like my tie eh?' He starts stuffing it into Harrison's mouth. 'BESAME MUNCHO! BESAME MUNCHO!!!' It was then that I realised it was nearly 10pm and if the session ran over management would kick up a fuss. I tapped Martin on the shoulder as he was forcing the last inch of tie into Harrison's mouth.

As soon as he saw the time he climbed off Harrison's chest, shook the boys' hands and sent them on their way with a promise to be in touch about a follow-up session. I remember Harrison walking out of there with Martin's tie still stuffed in his mouth. I wonder if he ever gave it back?

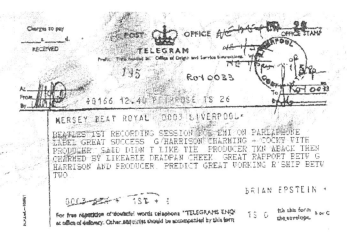

Charges to pay
____ s. ____ d.
RECEIVED

POST OFFICE OFFICE STAMP

TELEGRAM

145   ROY 0033

A:
From:
By: +G166 12.40 PRIMROSE TS 26

MERSEY BEAT ROYAL 0003 LIVERPOOL

BEATLES 1ST RECORDING SESSION FOR EMI ON PARLAPHONE
LABEL GREAT SUCCESS G/HARRISON CHARMING - COCKY VITH
PRODUCER SAID DIDN T LIKE TIE PRODUCER TKN ABACK THEN
CHARMED BY LIKEABLE DEADPAN CHEEK GREAT RAPPORT BETW G
HARRISON AND PRODUCER PREDICT GREAT WORKING R'SHIP BETW
TWO

BRIAN EPSTEIN +

0003   +   1ST + !

For free repetition of doubtful words telephone "TELEGRAMS ENQ"
at office of delivery. Other enquiries should be accompanied by this form

TS 0   this form
     this envelope.

[6]

In felawshipe and Beatles were they alle,
   Me thinketh it acordaunt to recall,
   George Martin (spoken with hem everichon)
   As to the layout of yon microphon.
   Embrouded was he, in the prettye dress,
   As fitting to the '50s as I gesse,
   Enquiring as to what they may dislyke,
   Up spake the smallest of them, but a tyke!
   'Your tie,' quoth he, and that fab compaignye,
   Didst roar as they were in a hostelrye.

Of Martin tho it pleaseth me to wryte,
   Knew songes they could make and wel endyte,
   So laughed as meekly as he were a mous,
   And 13 studio albums did produce.

Chaucer, *The Balance Engineer's Tale*

[7]

GEORGE MARTIN: I said to them: 'You've heard a lot from me. Now, is there anything you don't like?' George Harrison looked at me and said 'Yeah, I...' and at that moment a wasp flew in the control room door and began buzzing around his head, really persistently. He sort of shrieked and started thrashing his hands around to get rid of it. Paul said 'No George – the best thing is to stay still!' but he didn't seem to be listening. John, typical John [LAUGHS] said 'Squash the bugger!' Pete stayed at the back, still as a statue. And this blasted wasp just won't leave George alone. Possibly he had something in his hair which attracted it, I don't know. In the end Norman Smith used a soldering iron to frighten it off – it landed on the mixing console and Brian Epstein I think it was, clomped a great heavy tape box down on in – the session tape in fact.

When all the commotion had died down I said 'Sorry George, you were saying?' and he said 'I...I was just saying...I don't like your...tie' then he sort of tailed off. It was all a bit awkward really.

[8]

NORMAN SMITH: After they'd finished playing, Mr Paramor got them up to the control room for a chat; this was something he usually did, to be fair. He said they'd need to get some better equipment if they wanted to cut the mustard as recording artistes, then he took issue with their songs, saying he had some of his own compositions which would fit them well - he'd pass some acetates to their manager. The band didn't really react during all this, just sat there and listened. At the end of it all, Norrie said 'You've heard a lot from me. Is there anything you don't like?' George Harrison took a long look at him and said 'Yeah, I don't like your tie.' There was a bit of a pause, then Norrie said 'No, I mean anything you don't like about what I've just said, or about the work we've done today.' George didn't know what to say – he sort of looked round at the others, you know 'Back me up here, fellas!' By this time Norrie had got a bit of a bee in his bonnet.

'What's wrong with my tie anyway? It's just a tie; I've got to wear one to work and this is the one I happened to put on this morning. Why's it important what my tie's like? You should be wondering whether I can help you put out a record, not critiquing my neckwear.'

It was a pretty rocky start between them I can tell you, but as history shows Norrie took charge of the lads, knocked them into shape and gave them a string of hits we all know, including Play It Cool, The World Around Me and of course What's On Your Mind. Classic stuff.

[9]

GEORGE MARTIN: Then George said 'Yeah – I don't like your tie!' I just looked back at him. I tried not to show it, but every fibre of my being was vibrating with excitement. No one at EMI had ever picked up on it, but I wore that tie for every meeting with a new act.

I'd had the idea back in '58: I'd wear something to provoke a reaction and see if anyone...reacted. When you're in my position, you're looking for people to make a hit record with, but also people you might want to make a longer-term commitment to. What I was looking for was a spirit of...I was never sure actually, but I always felt I'd know it when I saw it.

I spent three weekends in 1959 combing the department stores, looking for the right thing.

At the end of the third weekend I saw it – hanging there by itself on a rail in Liberty's. No one had wanted it, it seems.

I spent a while looking at it from different angles. It really was absolutely awful. Unpleasant mix of colours, with a pretty unappealing horse motif. Looked sort of pompous but also seedy at the same time. I bought it immediately.

I wore it the following day and...nothing. For almost three years not a peep from anyone. I could see people looking at it with distaste, and on one or two occasions someone looked like they might be about to say something; Jim Dale came close, and possibly Bernard Cribbins. But not one of them looked at the monstrosity around my neck and had the guts to say 'What ARE you wearing?' No one until 6th June 1962.

[10]

RINGO: I'd been in the band about three months and we went into the studio to record From Me To You, I think it was. At the end we listened back in the control room and George Martin said you know, 'How does the mix sound – anything you don't like?' Then George says 'I don't like your tie' and him, Paul, John and George Martin fall about laughing. I didn't get it – the tie was ok you know? Just a tie. I didn't like to ask what was funny...still felt like the 'new boy' at that point. The thing is, it kept happening over the years. Someone would ask us if we didn't like anything, George would say the tie thing and the three of them would be in hysterics. It happened with Richard Lester, Michael Lyndsay-Hogg, Maharishi.

By mid-1969 I'd decided that next time George said 'I don't like your tie' I'd ask the three of them what was so funny about it, but...it didn't happen.

[11]

GEORGE MARTIN: I must say after that first encounter with The Beatles I didn't think about ties all that much for a good while – things seemed to happen so fast after that. In addition to a pretty intense recording and release schedule I also ended up writing the scores for the A Hard Day's Night and Yellow Submarine films, along with various other activities. It must have been about 1968 before I had chance to stop, catch my breath as it were, and realise I'd never once seen George wearing a tie since that day back in June 1962. I started to wonder if he just didn't like ties generally and that's why he reacted to mine so strongly. Then one day in January 1969 I went to the Apple studio on Savile Row to see how work on the Get Back project's going and the first thing I see is George, wearing...let me try and describe it: imagine the kind of velvet bow tie you'd see on an eight-year-old at their first violin recital, or a teddy bear at Hamleys.

That's what George was wearing; the most ludicrous, taste-less tie I have ever seen in my life. Where had it come from? Why, after seven years of no ties had he chosen to re-enter the world of the tie with...*that*?

Michael's film cameras were rolling of course so I didn't say anything but at one point while they were running through For You Blue I made eye contact with George and he just grinned at me and winked.

[12]

GEORGE MARTIN: So after I'd been on at them for quite a while I said 'Listen, you've heard a lot from me. Is there anything you don't like?' George Harrison looked straight at me and said 'Well for starters, is this an audition or a contracted recording session? Brian's telegram said he'd got us a recording contact and he signed and returned the contract you sent him last month but he's not received your signed copy yet.' Then Paul piped up: 'And what's all this about you only getting us in because Ardmore and Beechwood want the publishing on PS I Love You?' Before I could even think, John came at me: 'And what if you don't like any of our songs and want us to do some Tin Pan Alley rubbish – can we tell you where to go?' Then Pete, who hadn't said a word up to this point, spoke up from the back: 'I know you generally prefer to cut new groups' records using session drummers. Is that something you'll be looking to do on this record?'

There was a bit of a silence after this, I must say. Then George looked up at me from under his fringe and said 'Nice tie, by the way.'

[13]

At the end of the session I remember George Martin asked if there was anything they didn't like. He was reaching for an eclair, so had his back to them when it happened: someone very clearly said: '*I don't like your tie.*'

'Who said that?' he asked. No answer. He was calm, but persistent. 'Come on. Who said it?' It was clear nothing would happen until the culprit was found. What made it more awkward was the fact I was taking a tour of the studio with my Aunt Jane who was visiting from St Mary Mead.

In an effort to dispel the tension we all went down to the canteen. Aunt Jane sat there very quietly, watching, as she does. At exactly 9pm, she said she must be getting off to bed.

It was at that point she mentioned that Mr Lennon's unfortunate reluctance to wear spectacles despite his obvious short sightedness suggested he could barely see the tie to make an assessment. And that the dried chocolate stain on Mr McCartney's arm was an indication he too had reached for an eclair, placing him close enough to Mr Martin as to remove all doubt, had he said it.

As for the percussionist Mr Best, she suggested he had a quiet nature, so he was hardly likely to make such a forthright declaration.

It only really left one possibility. She looked at him over her tea cup. 'Wouldn't you agree... Mr Harrison?'

Audition for Death, 1962, Agatha Christie

[14]

AL: How would you describe your relationship with George Harrison?

RAVI: Our friendship reverberates clearly, even today. Our first formal collaboration was the Concert for Bangladesh in 1971, but we had met in the '60s. George was fascinated by ragas and you can see the influence on Love You To. I think he was looking for... a deeper dimension to his playing.

AL: Did he ever mention the incident with George Martin's tie?

RAVI: I would rather not discuss this.

[TAPE STOPS]

[TAPE RESUMES]

RAVI: (INAUDIBLE) —-working together. I will say this. George's interest in the sitar and the Indian classical tradition brought with it his first real period of internal reflection. Regrets, mistakes. Things came to the surface. Rarely could we complete a lesson without him saying something like. '*I feel awful. Looking back, the tie wasn't so bad.'* Or... '*I wouldn't mind but my own tie was pretty average.'* Even '*Bloody hell Ravi, it could have been a present from his wife. What was I thinking?'* It was kind of difficult. When he arrived, he said he had wanted to come to India with The Beatles because fewer people wore ties here so there was less chance of being reminded of what he'd said. I explained that was nonsense. India was the second most populous country in the world – half a billion people. I told him there were probably more ties in India than in the UK. He went very pale. The only regret I have about the entire visit, was the gift I gave him when he landed. It was a tie.

Ravi Shankar, *Rolling Stone* interview, August 2008

[15]

GEORGE MARTIN: So they finished playing, put down their instruments and made their way up to the control room. Magic Alex was tinkering with some kind of light box when he should have been re-spooling the tapes but I let that pass. Once they were settled I'll admit I gave them a bit of a talking to, about their playing and their choice of material and... pretty much everything really. Their minder Horst looked like he was about to take a pop at me to be honest. But they listened, to be fair to them. I finished by saying I'd only really given them a hearing because their manager Mr Klein had been so...persuasive. All through it they just sat there, John messing with his beard, Paul fiddling with his quiff, the drummer – Norman I think, just head down, saying nothing. At the end of it all I said 'You've heard a lot from me. Is there anything you don't like?' and George looked at me, put down what I'm pretty such was a reefer. and said 'Yeah, I don't dig...' but at that moment a voice called out 'Your tie! I don't like your tie!' We'd all quite forgotten Yoko was still in her bed down on the studio floor. [LAUGHS]

[16]

GEORGE MARTIN: 6th June 1962 – a day I'll always remember. At lunchtime in the canteen it was salmon with new potatoes and Hollandaise sauce - Sir Joseph must have had someone important in. I was in the middle of eating, first-rate it was, and I looked down at my plate and one of the potatoes looked *just* like Peter Sellers. I'd worked with him a fair amount of course, so he was often on my mind to some extent. But this potato looked SO much like him pulling one of those ridiculous faces he used to do. I just started laughing. People began to look around at me so I managed to stifle it, but then I looked back down at this potato, peering up at me though the Hollandaise, and it set me off again. In the end I had to abandon the meal and go for a walk around the block to calm down. That evening I caught the tail-end of The Beatles session, then got them up to the control room for a bit of a chat. I'd done this kind of thing scores of times before with new acts so I was on auto-pilot really. At the point I always reached, where I'd say 'Anything you don't like?' there was the usual awkward silence and right in the middle of it I suddenly remembered the potato that looked like Peter Sellers. One of the Beatles said something to me, I didn't catch it because I was just seeing the potato in my mind's eye, glaring up at me from the plate...and I'm afraid I just burst out laughing.

The strange thing was, they started laughing as well. I've no idea why. After that we all carried on chatting and things were much more natural. I think as long as I live I shall never forget that day – the day I saw the potato that looked like Peter Sellers.

[17]

Tune-In, Mark Lewisohn (Little, Brown and Company RRP £19.99)

When an advance copy of this book landed on my desk I must confess I felt a small thrill of excitement; according to its blurb the work deals with 'one of the greatest entertainment phenomena of the sixties'. As all Tie Monthly readers will know, the 1960s were the beginning of the last great age of tie-wearing in this country, so a book set in that decade (and over 800 pages to boot!) must surely be rich in detail for tie-loving bibliophiles?

It gives me no pleasure to report that this is not the case. The book, which deals in excruciating detail with the rise of a provincial pop group, barely mentions ties of any kind, much less provides any serious insight into the role of neckwear in that most fashion-conscious of decades. (And, to pre-empt the deluge of letters I am certain to receive, Lewisohn's occasional mentions of teddy boy 'boot-lace ties' do not count, as these are not ties in any meaningful sense. *) Indeed, any mention of ties in the text is all but buried under an avalanche of extraneous detail about the day-to-day activities of the members of the pop group and their efforts to achieve success in the music industry.

My flagging interest threatened to revive briefly about three quarters of the way through when one of the pop group criticises the tie of a record producer, but no additional detail is conveyed as to the substance of this critique, and the pattern and provenance of the tie itself is dispatched in a mere nine words. I cannot in all good conscience recommend this book to the readers of Tie Monthly.

Those interested in the evolution of neckwear during the nineteen sixties would be better advised to track down a copy of Ian MacDonald's 'Revolution Round the Neck', a far superior work in every regard.

Tie Monthly Oct 2013, Vol 89, No 15

*see Vol 87, Nos 4-15 for extensive, and conclusive, discussion on this.

[18]

Moving on to scene 34 (pgs 16-18); the 'tie' scene... It's really great, really gets across the feel of the band's 'big break' and you're right, the whole narrative arc definitely needs *something* at this point but...we're just not sure this is it. A few 'starters for ten': (a) If you're going to have a scene with only two speaking parts, they can't both be called George. We imagine you're wedded to the guitarist being 'George', but the producer character's pretty much a bit part – something else perhaps? Harry? Dave? Something to think about. (b) We're not altogether clear about motivations in this scene – does the producer character like these 'Beatles' or not? Seems a bit hot and cold tbh. Some clarity would be helpful here. (c) He's laying into them and they just sit there and...take it? In the previous fifteen pages you've shown us this badass, edgy band. Stealing instruments, beating up sailors, setting fire to cinemas. No audience is going to believe these guys just sit there and get told off like a bunch of schoolboys. Finally (d) You're not going to like this, but...we're really not happy about the punchline. 'I don't like your tie'. We just don't get it. Structurally it's like you're building to a great line here, something which makes sense of the whole scene and then...one guy doesn't like another guy's tie? As soon as 'George' says that line all the momentum just goes. We're not writers obviously, and wouldn't tell you how to do your job, but maybe something along the lines of 'So are you gonna make us stars then, Dave?' You'll be able to punch it up obviously, but that's the kind of thing we had in mind. The rest of it's great though – really strong stuff. Speak soon.

[19]

GEORGE MARTIN: The Anthology project was a great time, a real pleasure to be collaborating with the boys again. I worked closely with the documentary's producer Geoff Wonfor, making sure the right versions of songs were used in each episode, and selecting outtakes, studio chatter, that sort of thing. I remember we'd just finished the rough cut of episode one, which covers from the earliest days right up to the release of Love Me Do, and we got Paul, George and Ringo down to the edit suite for a watch-through. At the end I said to them 'So boys, anything you don't like?' There was a bit of a silence, then George Harrison said 'Well for starters I don't like "I don't like your tie."' He explained that he thought everyone was sick of that story now and could we take it out. I remember saying to him, 'I *like* "I don't like your tie."' But George quite rightly had the final say and we took it out. A week later the boys came back to approve the project's promotional material, part of which featured footage of them watching that rough cut the previous week. When it finished I said to them 'So boys, anything you don't like?' There was a bit of a silence then George Harrison said 'Well for starters I don't like "Well for starters I don't like 'I don't like your tie'"'. Then he paused and looked at my neck. 'And by the way, I don't like your tie.'

[20]

The 1962 BBC series *'Band Chance'* can be safely said to be the progenitor of what we now know as 'structured reality television'.

The 21-part series followed the fortunes of acts like The Tommy Parbold Four, The Quick Geoffreys and The Beatles. The bands performed and completed a series of challenges under the withering eye of chairman George Martin and fellow judges Ken Townsend and Norman Smith.

The brainchild of Director General Hugh Carleton Greene, the show made full use of the innovative new handheld Evershed Power Optics cameras, which could be comfortably transported by three large men, making it effectively television's first 'fly-on-the-wall' show.

Each week viewers were able to vote via postcard for the act they thought should survive to the next round - with the losing band agreeing to return to their factory jobs. The winners would receive an EMI record contract and seven pounds.

Beatle guitarist George Harrison looked to be impressing viewers with a heartfelt plea that his band should go through, because it was his dream and his nan had died recently. But a catastrophic 'joke' concerning Mr Martin's tie saw viewers vote the Liverpudlian band off in week 12.

The clip of the outraged George Martin sounding his air horn, standing, buttoning his jacket and walking silently from the studio was electrifying television – wittily evoked in Season 10 Episode 18 of Below Deck (Bravo, 2013 -) when Andy confronts Captain Lee about his cravat.

The Quick Geoffreys survived to the final, but the shock reintroduction of The Tommy Parbold Four from week nine saw the eventual creation of The Four Geoffreys – and the rest is history.

***The BBC: A People's History 1959 – 64*, David Hendy**

[21]

Little did I know it but my new job at EMI was soon to change my life. One day I was sweeping the front steps and these four mop-top youths came in; I could tell at once there was something special about them. As they walked past I assessed them in turn: sarcastic John, diplomatic Paul, spiritual George and shy Pete. I could tell they found a kindred spirit in me; another rough, working-class man trying to make his way in the world.

'Eh up mate!' John said. 'We're here to see George Martin!' Quick as a flash, I quipped 'Nice to see you've made an effort with your haircuts!' I could tell they were all impressed. As we stood there, me with my brush in my hand, they with their guitars and drums, I broke the silence with another gag: 'Wait 'til you see Mr Martin's tie. Someone should have a word with him about it!'

'Hmmm…maybe I will!' said George, and of course we know what happened next.

Over the years I was to become a confidante of all the band, one of the 'inner circle'. They even had a nickname for me; 'Len' they'd call me.

[21]

'Hello er...Len' John would say as he passed me sweeping up reception at the end of the day. I'll never forget the time Paul was looking for lyric ideas for one of his songs...

***'Our Len': The Beatles and Me*, Len Moulton, Alma Books 1997**

[22]

PETE BEST: Then George Martin says to us 'Is there anything you don't like?' He probably didn't notice but we all tensed up a bit at this. You see we'd been pretty sure he'd ask something like that and the other three had been keen to have something to say back to him. Something funny, y'know. For about three weeks before we went down to the recording session they'd been brainstorming lines. All the time backstage at gigs, in the van, even when we were just walking down the street. John, Paul and George just constantly trying to come up with a good, memorable line to put in if George Martin asked 'Anything you don't like?' They went through so many ideas; at one point, John was going to say 'Yes, your ears are too tall', and for a while they were all keen on one where Paul would say 'Yeah, me Auntie Gin always burns the soup.' In the end I remember it was literally a day or two before we were due to travel down to London, we were in the Cavern rehearsing what songs we were going to do and they were still on at it, couldn't make their minds up and I just said 'What about "I don't like your tie"?' They all looked at me, then burst out laughing. It's not often I'd make them laugh so it really stuck with me. They just loved that line.

I'm nervous though, quite happy drumming but never keen on
speaking up so we decided George would say it. Good line, that.

[23]

I think I'd been involved in covert operations for say... 12 years? I'd been in signals in the war, top-secret at the time but fine to talk about it now. After that I was picked up by The Security Service. You'd probably know it as MI5.

Around 1968 I went freelance – doing one-off covert surveillance jobs for high-end clients. Early 1969 I got a call from a man called Michael Lindsay-Hogg who wanted to install a covert film camera in the reception of Apple at Savile Row for some filming event or other. Now given a day, two days, access to my kit, I could have done it properly, but he was saying *'Today! Today! It has to be today!'* I did the best I could, but it was a big bloody box on the desk. Hopeless.

Well obviously it was a disaster. George Martin comes in and clocks it straight away, and he's just grinning. Outright laughing at it. What a farrago. I decided to go up top and just watch the band. Bloody freezing it was.

After the gig they were all very happy, so I got talking to George Martin. He was still chuckling away about that camera set-up, *'wouldn't fool anyone'* – all that. Professionally I was... put out. So I told him something...

See, it wasn't the first time our paths had crossed. 'I did some work at EMI in '62,' I said. 'The boss there, Sir Joseph, he

36

36

didn't quite trust the producers. Wanted to keep an eye on the auditions. Did you know there was a fake side on your control desk?' Well obviously his face fell. So I finished my drink. 'We kept a good eye on you Mr Martin. George over there was right. That tie was bloody awful.'

Marty Foster, Security Service (Retired), *At the Sharp End. My life in Intelligence.*

[24]

GEORGE HARRISON: So George Martin asks us if there's anything we don't like and I say 'I don't like your tie.' Ever since we'd got up to the control room and been introduced to him that was the only thing I'd been able to think about. I don't know why, and I know it sounds ridiculous, but something about his tie made me very uncomfortable; like a really deep, irrational aversion. So I just blurted it out: 'I don't like your tie.' Of course as you'll have heard, he laughed like it was the funniest thing ever, then the others all joined in and that was the start of it for us and him. I tried to put it out of my mind and things were fine after that, but then one day in it was probably May 1966 I come into the studio and he's got that tie on again. And that same feeling rises in me and all I can do is turn around and go home. That was the day we were due to record For No One, which is why I'm not on it. The same thing happened a few more times in the following years – I'm not on stuff like Don't Pass Me By, Good Night and a few others. Always the tie. When it came to Free As A Bird in '94 I couldn't risk seeing it again so I told Paul and Ringo I'd only do it if we could use Jeff Lynne. He wore a tie, but it was a nice one.

[25]

𒈗 𒂊𒆠 𒋾𒂊𒄑𒐊𒊏 𒋼𒂊𒄑𒐊𒐊𒋾𒌋𒐊𒀸𒈨 𒌋𒄿𒆠 𒀭𒅗 𒐊𒊑𒈨𒌋𒌋𒈨 𒌑𒒊 𒉿𒆤𒈨𒄿𒐊

𒂊𒆠 𒐊𒄿𒈪𒂊𒄑𒆠 𒐊𒊏𒐊 𒂊𒆠𒉿𒈪𒐊𒐊 𒊑𒐊𒆠 𒄿𒂊𒆤𒂊𒂅𒐊𒋰𒐊𒑊

𒉿𒋿 𒂊𒆠𒐊𒊑𒐊𒀸𒉿𒌋 𒐊𒀸𒌉𒂠𒐊𒉿𒈪𒄿𒅀 𒌋𒈨𒐊𒆤𒂊𒑊

𒌋𒈨𒆠 𒐊𒋾𒈨𒊏𒄿𒅖𒄿 𒌑𒀀 𒌋𒈨𒐊𒑊 𒂊𒄿𒋢𒋾𒌋𒈨𒐊𒂅 𒐊𒋾𒂊𒆤 𒌋𒈨𒆠

𒌋𒈨𒆠 𒐊𒄿𒈨𒂊𒂊𒐊 𒐊𒊏𒑊 𒄿𒌋𒑊𒐊 𒂊𒆠𒄑𒂅𒐊 𒌋𒈨𒆠 𒋢𒐊𒀸𒂊𒐊𒑊 𒄿𒄿𒐊𒊏

𒌋𒈨𒆠 𒐊𒂊𒆤𒂊𒂅𒐊𒋰𒐊𒑊 𒂊𒆠𒑊𒉿𒄑𒐊𒐊𒐊 𒐊𒐊𒂊𒐊𒄿𒄿𒆠 𒌋𒈨𒐊𒑊

𒐊𒂊𒂊𒑊𒐊𒐊𒐊𒐊𒐊 𒋾𒐊 𒌋𒐊 𒌋𒈨𒆠 𒐊𒂊𒆠𒉿𒉿𒐊𒈨 𒂊𒊏𒄑𒐊𒐊 𒌑𒑊 𒑊𒂊𒐊𒈨𒐊𒆠

Cuneiform tablet, c.2100 BCE Mesopotamia

39

[26]

GEORGE MARTIN: At the end of all this I said to them 'You've heard a lot from me. Is there anything you're not happy about?' There was a bit of a silence then George Harrison said 'Yeah. I don't like your tie.' John said 'Oh God, not this' and sort of put his head in his hands. 'What?' I asked.

'George has written this song' Paul said. 'And it's called...' 'I Don't Like Your Tie' finished George. 'We've done three of John and Paul's songs. We've even done flippin' Besame Mucho. What about MY song?'

As it happened there were still 20 minutes of the session left, so I told them to go back down and run through it. I've got to say, the other members of the group didn't look too happy about all this – John was looking daggers at George as they went back down and Paul was muttering to himself.

But in a few minutes they were ready. Norman put a new tape on the machine and off they went.

The strange thing is, 'I Don't Like Your Tie' was so much better than the three other originals they'd played me. Catchy tune, really interesting chords, great lyrics; heartfelt but also funny. A smashing song. Sadly once they'd left it turned out there was some fault with the machine and it hadn't recorded.

George didn't bring another song into the studio until You Know What To Do in mid-1964. I always intended to come back to I Don't Like Your Tie but they never mentioned it again.

[27]

What I Did At The Weekend

This weekend was donkey day in the park it is every year and there are rides for 5/- which mum says is robbery also you can feed them. It is one time a year. We went to the seaside last summer and there were donkeys there all the time but in the park they are just one time a year and it is donkey day. My dad came with us he is an engineer in a record studio he has met tommy steel and got me anautograph of tommy steel. He told a joke that had happened to him at work in the week. A pop group came to do songs and one said I don't like your tie he did not say it to my dad he said it to my dads boss but dads boss did not mind he laughed. I did not think it was funny.

Dad said maybe I had to be there. But I was not. He was happy though and got me an extra ride on the donkey it was called Fancy

Billy Smith Class 2

[28]

GEORGE MARTIN: At the end of it all I said to them, 'Is there anything you don't like?' One of the George Harrisons looked at me and 'Yeah, I don't like your tie.' I remembered what Brian had told me: one George Harrison always lied, one always told the truth. If this George Harrison was telling the truth then what he'd said was an insult, the kind that could sink a working relationship before it had even begun. Alternatively, if he was lying then it was an irreverent joke of the kind that would charm me immensely. I remembered the other thing Brian had said: 'You can only ask one of the George Harrisons one question.' I racked my brains, then it came to me. I looked at the George Harrison who'd spoken and asked him 'If I asked the other George Harrison if he liked my tie, what would he say?' The George Harrison looked back at me. 'He'd say... he doesn't like your tie.' After a bit of a think I burst into laughter and the rest of the session went like a dream. From then on things ran very smoothly with the boys... until the day Brian announced they'd be travelling to their February 1964 Big Night Out appearance by boat, along with a chicken, a fox and a bag of grain.

[29]

GEORGE HARRISON: I remember the trip to EMI pretty well, yeah. We get to the studio, set up and we're about to start when one of us, John probably, says to the engineer 'So where's this George Martin?' Cos that was the name we had – he was the one Brian had met and all that. The engineer said Mr Martin was in the canteen but they'd fetch him if they needed to. So we started running through the songs we'd prepared. It all sounded ok but when we got to Love Me Do it turned out John had forgotten his harmonica. He must have left it at the hotel. We had a discussion – should we do it anyway, or go on to the next one? In the end I said the harmonica was such an important part of that song it wouldn't work without it. So we moved onto PS I Love You or whatever it was. All through it the engineer's watching us – taps his foot occasionally but no sign of fetching Mr Martin. In the end we went through everything we'd planned to do, apart from Love Me Do obviously, packed up our gear and left. As we were on the way out we bumped into George Martin in the corridor – didn't say more than a few words to him really. I remember he had this awful tie on.

[29]

Anyway Brian got a telegram a few days later saying Parlophone wouldn't be taking up the option of recording the other sides and we were free to look elsewhere. So that's how we ended up on Fontana. Which... they were ok, you know? They were fine.

[30]

KEN TOWNSEND: I'm pretty sure that by the time the session took place the Autobot Beatle Leadership Matrix had passed to John. It had been difficult for the lads obviously, four million years asleep, waking up on a new world, getting to grips with their new alternative forms.

And there was no ill-feeling between our two races - despite the fact that on arriving at the studio John, in jet mode, had obliterated George Martin's Vauxhall Victor. Paul was so embarrassed by this he had turned into a car and was off. If I remember correctly he was a Ford Cortina. 1100 Deluxe.

George wanted them to feel at home, so he offered thanks to their god Primus, and sympathised with them about the recent outbreak of Scraplets in Norris Green. Simple, friendly stuff. But when he asked if there was anything they didn't like, George Harrison said: 'I don't like your tie.'

Well they all stood there laughing, big metal shoulders bouncing up and down for absolutely ages. We let it go, because they were such good company. For the rest of the session George Harrison just sat there. As an EMI TR-90 tape machine.

[31]

As soon as the Hell's Angels turned up we knew we were in for a rough time. I don't think George meant for them to literally *live* at Savile Row, but that's what they did. We were all mindful of George's memo saying 'don't uptight them' but after the fracas at the Christmas party everyone wanted them to leave. It turned out so did The Beatles, even George, but no one wanted to face up to these enormous, brutish Americans and tell them to shove off. In the end George knew he had to be the one. One morning late in December he came into the main office, which is where they'd set up their base. All of us in there could feel the atmosphere the second he walked in. Even someone as dumb as Frisco Pete sensed something was up – he got up from where he was lounging and stood toe-to-toe with George. Towering over him he was. So George looks up at him, staring really intently in his eyes and says quietly 'I don't like your tie.'

Now Frisco Pete, as is the case with most Hell's Angels, isn't wearing a tie. But he still kind of involuntarily looks down at his chest. Then back at George, with a sort of 'What???' look on his face. George does nothing. Just keeps looking at him. 'I don't like your tie.'

Another long pause. Frisco Pete gulps, so loud we all hear it. George keeps staring at him. 'I don't like your tie.' They were out of the place in five minutes.

Derek Taylor, *Fifty Years Adrift*, Genesis, 1983

[32]

I was lucky to have an encounter with George last year. I am from Argentina and my wife and I took our honeymoon in England. We travelled to Liverpool of course and saw the site of the Cavern and even met Allan Williams! Then we went to London to Paul's house at Cavendish Avenue (he was away), Liberty (I bought a tie!) and the balcony at EMI House (we took a photo leaning over it like on Please Please Me!) On our last day we took a bus to Henley hoping to find Friar Park. We asked at a pub and the owner told us where it was. When we got to the lodge I knocked on the door. We were surprised when George's brother Harry opened the door! He said George was busy in the house. We told him we had come from Argentina, and had brought some traditional dolls from our country for baby Dhani. Harry went into the lodge and made a phone call. Then he told us George would see us! We were very excited. We went with Harry through the big gates. When we got close to the house a man stepped out from behind a bush and I thought it to be a gardener – he had a big brown hat and soil on his clothes. My wife knew before I did that it was George! He said hello. We gave him the dolls and he said he would give them to Dhani! He was so polite and caring. George asked us about Argentina. When we said this was our honeymoon he said 'Congratulations!' He laughed when we told him about Allan Williams. 'I'll have to be getting back now' he said. We thanked him for his generous time with us. We shook hands. As he was leaving he turned round and looked at me. 'I like your tie' he said.

Anonymous contribution, *Harrison Alliance* magazine, March 1979

[33]

The men worked and as they worked the sound never stopped. The glass moving and clinking, sometimes smashing. When break time came the men gathered at the back of the main shed and smoked. Cold night for June. Overhead the gulls halloohalloohalloohallo'd. Smokes and mugs of tea from the canteen. Mugs went missing. Management said they'd not buy any more. Foreman said his dog had gone missing. One man asked who was going the match. Two men were. Apart from that they smoked. One man sucked tea noisily through stumpy front teeth. He didn't speak, just looked up at the seagulls. Downhearted. Someone asked him what was up. He was always a miserable sod but even worse tonight. Don't know he said. Don't know. Noisy tea. Slender fingers rolled a smoke. Lit up. Coughed. More gulls gathered overhead. Then. A perfect still silence for one, two, three seconds. halloohalloohalloohalloo the gulls burst out laughing. Foreman looks at his watch. Time he says. Time. Come on. Stamps out his smoke and goes back into the shed with his empty mug. The other men follow him. Come on Moore he says, those bottles won't make themselves.

[34]

JEREMY PAXMAN: *Ha Ha Mr Wilson. Ha Ha Mr Heath* – so sang The Beatles in the song *Taxman*. Well could it soon be a case of *Ha Ha Mr Harrison*? The former Beatle's support for The Natural Law Party, culminating in a Royal Albert Hall gig last night, has led to a surprise poll boost for the mystic yogic flyers. And they could be on the verge of an upset as Mr Harrison assumes control of the party following what some insiders are calling a 'coup'. George Harrison, how exactly will bouncing along on your bottom on a big mattress create jobs?

HARRISON: Well we'll need more mattresses.

PAXMAN: And what do you, a millionaire in a mansion, have in common with the vast majority of working men and women in this country?

HARRISON: Legs?

PAXMAN: Does that old '60s interview schtick really wash now? You used to be known as 'The quiet Beatle'? You're not that quiet about personal freedoms, are you? Freedom of choice when it comes to... neckwear.

HARRISON: This issue is precisely why I've taken the action I have. I intend to reshape our manifesto to take a position on dubious, some might say 'offensive' neckwear. We've been labouring under the egregiously ill-thought-out 'poll' tax, have we not? When it first entered our language in the 13th century of course the word 'poll' meant someone's head. And who's to say one shouldn't speak up when an egregiously ill-thought-out accessory is established not far from a head?

PAXMAN: Should a former pop star...

HARRISON: Please, let me finish. The rank, base inadequacy of many ties has for too long created a literal stranglehold around the neck of the British -

PAXMAN: And the bouncing?

HARRISON: I HAVEN'T FINISHED. FOUR YOUNG MUSICIANS, CONFRONTED WITH... THAT! How can it be right Jeremy? HOW CAN IT BE FAIR? HOW CAN IT BE FAIR?

PAXMAN: And now a quick look at the papers...

BBC Archive. Newsnight BBC 2, 7th April 1992.

[35]

I met a traveller from an antique band,
    Who said – 'One long and shapeless strip of silk
    Hangs in the studio... Near it, by the desk,
    Half cut, a famed producer lies, whose shirt,
    And trouser crease and finely parted hair,
    Betray his sense of hurt sartorial pride.
    His '50s style, and fashionable report,
    Now savaged by this youngest Beatle, George.
    And on the session tape these words appear:
    "My name is George H Martin, King of Kings;
    Look on my Works ye Mighty and despair!"
    Around him, albums lie. Those records spake:
    Jim Dale. The Temperance Seven.
    Bernard Cribbins. Charlie Drake.'

Percy Bysshe Shelley

[36]

GEORGE HARRISON: Growing up with the name George Har-rison wasn't easy. My parents, Dave and June Harrison were quite particular people. They didn't know who The Beatles were because they were terrified of the radio. Something about the waves. Mum's dad was called George, so that's where I got the name. They were none the wiser. I have a vivid recollection of the first time, primary school, Martin Henshaw saying: 'What – George Harrison - like the Beatle?'

I've always hated them.

I'm A Walrus. Yellow Submarine. Look It's Sunny Again. They're... nursery rhymes for morons. When I finally got the chance to listen to music I lost myself in Francisco Tarrega, Roland Dyens, Heitor Villa-Lobos. The classical guitar really suited me. But I could never practise. It would start every time anyone saw me with a guitar. '*Do you need any Help, George? Is it gently weeping?*' Idiots.

I was a bit of a loner. This was the late '70s and I probably would have worn some more interesting clothes, let my hair grow, maybe a moustache, but no. I suppose I was trying to create some distance from... him.

Setting up the tie shop was pretty much the worst thing I could've done. I had no idea. I started hearing the joke a few months in, but I'd committed the money by then. I probably hear it a few times a month. I need the sale so I just smile.

Change it? I thought about it. It would really upset my mum. It wasn't her fault.

BBC Archive Extract: The People's Century. October 13 1988.

[37]

FOR IMMEDIATE RELEASE: Apple Corps, Wingnut Films, Walt Disney Studios confirm 2025 streaming event: 'The Long and Winding Tie.'

Peter Jackson, Wellington, NZ:

'I'm so excited to be bringing this project to you. As a lifelong Beatle nut I'm used to all the "what ifs?", but this is the big one. What tie was George Harrison actually talking about?

'Well, six months ago a BBC archive assistant unearthed footage shot at EMI on 6th June 1962 by a film crew who had arrived to interview Sir Joseph Lockwood.

'Remarkably the film crew also shot a couple of seconds' footage through the window into Studio 2's control room, capturing the exact moment when George Harrison made his remark and featuring a few frames where the tie itself is clearly visible.

'Technologically this project wouldn't have been possible even a year ago. Harnessing state-of-the-art AI and the latest digital compositing techniques we've been able to analyse Harrison's lip movements and the frames featuring George Martin to reproduce not only the original comment, but also the tie itself.

'The support of the remaining Beatles, Yoko, Olivia and the George Martin Tie Archive were the final pieces of the puzzle. I'm grateful to Giles Martin for allowing us to go on this journey. As a fan I'm as excited as you guys.'

Jackson added: 'What I hope to do is show that over the years there's been a lot of negativity attached to this comment. I've seen the rushes and you're in for a treat. There's a different story coming through.

Sure, George said what he said about the tie, but looking at some of this stuff now? I think he probably liked it.'

The Long and Winding Tie will be available to stream on Disney+ from August 2025.

Dur: 780 minutes.

[38]

The worlds of gaming and music align this week with the release of the Beatles edition of the blockbuster Rockband series (Rockstar, RRP49.99).

The game starts in 1961 with the Fab Four's first trip to Hamburg, playing eight-hour sets to rowdy German audiences. The tasks on this level aren't all that challenging – the sailor is surprisingly easy to mug and the condom nailed to the cinema wall catches fire pretty much on first attempt – but both present a chance to get the feel of the game, and soon you'll really feel you're one of the band.

The 1962 section is a little more challenging, especially when you reach the end-of-level-boss, George Martin. For this level you play as George Harrison, delivering the famous 'tie' line. Let me tell you, the game gives absolutely no quarter at this point. Too much Scouse drawl: fail. Not enough Scouse drawl: fail. Bolshy rather than cheeky: fail. Ingratiating rather than cocksure: fail. The sense of achievement when Martin's avatar begins to laugh is immense.

And the fun keeps coming – play the Manila Airport level with any vibrating gaming chair and you'll feel you're really being jostled and kicked by a dozen enraged Filipino customs officials.

In a nutshell, the whole game is a delight, from the intro screen right through to mastering John's arm controls to lob that brick through Paul's window.

Score: 98/100. Lost two points for slight blockiness in the Maharishi's Helicopter flight sim level.

PLAY *Magazine*, no.442 Feb 2009

[39]

Many are surprised when they learn that George Harrison *never actually said:* 'It isn't even the worst tie in The Beatles.'

It's commonly believed that the story was actually first related by Big Narstie on Channel Four's Big Fat Quiz of the Year 2015. But fewer people appreciate that having shared a writer in common, the brilliant story was actually told 18 months previously by Katherine Ryan in the first series of Eight out of Ten Cats Does Countdown.

Here the story gets rather more complicated. Represented by United Agents, Ryan was handled by the son of her press liaison Tandy Baxter – whose uncle Tom Follet originally represented Angus Deayton during his HIGNFY years. Most experts agree that it's ANGUS who, in 1994 first uttered the immortal line when panel member Sir Rhodes Boyson MP asked if George Martin's masculine neck adornment was the worst tie in the world. You know the rest.

But is that really where the story ends?

Recently a rewatch of the October 1989 third episode of Laurence Marks and Maurice Gran's *Birds of a Feather,* stopped me in my tracks. Sassy man-eater next door Dorien Green relates the EXACT SAME anecdote, but in relation to Tracey's husband not wearing the worst tie in HMP Slade (yes, SLADE).

And there, I thought, the case rests. But does it rest where I thought it was?

Last night, I'd settled down for a rewatch of Yorkshire Television's 1982 Peter Bowles vehicle *The Bounder,* when the impossible happened...

Geoff Belling, *The Beatles and Three of a Kind: A Common Purpose*, Fantom Publishing 2023

[40]

REDDIT GROUP: F@bFour:TieMen. Thread 348 11.48 6th June 2021.

JOSH 346: I can't quite believe it... but this is NEW. We've focused so hard on finding tape ops, reception staff - but think about it – EMI was a busy place and we KNOW there were repairs being done to Studio 3 next door that day [Big thanks to ILoveHurricaneSmith245 for unearthing those invoices!] Turns out some of the guys working in the corridor that day are still alive. Ted Marshall is 87 and he was THERE, working as a carpenter. Just fixing a door hinge on the day!!! Heard the whole thing!!! Off to see him will post later!!

18.48. New Post:

TED: God it was such a memorable day. I've never forgotten it.

JOSH 346: Go on!

TED: Well the hinge was pre-war! It went straight in the collection for my apprentice, Tom.

JOSH 346: How did you feel that day?

TED: I can't quite describe it to be honest.

JOSH 346: Overwhelming you mean?

TED: Absolutely. I mean to find a hinge like that. I think it was a repurposed from a cabinet – the craftsmanship was out of this world.

JOSH 346: Was there any discussion of a tie that day?

TED: Yes! God we were laughing!

JOSH 346: Fantastic! what happened?

TED: Well a tie line is the first thing you learn as a carpenter! And the mess Tom made of it! Unforgettable day. I was trying to set him straight but there was some band in. What a racket.

JOSH 346: That band...was The Beatles. Did you speak to any of them?

TED: Oh yes. About the hinge.

JOSH 346: (SILENCE) Which Beatle did you speak to?

TED: ...Stephen?

[41]

STATEMENT ISSUED ON BEHALF OF PAUL MCCARTNEY, 6th June 1968

Today, we look to the future. As we know, there has for many years been a member of The Beatles who had concerns about the tie worn by George Martin when we first joined the E.M.I. in 1962. For too long our tie-sceptic Beatle was ignored by Westminster and a London-centric media elite.

The result of the subsequent referendum, while unexpected, was clear. The Beatles had spoken. We wanted the tie to leave George Martin. It was my job to deliver on that overwhelming mandate. I pay tribute to EMI, George Martin, and his wife for today signing the Apple Accords, and in doing so, accepting the will of The Beatles.

There are of course, the naysayers. People who suggest that George Martin's ability to still regularly wear the tie represents some kind of failure on my part. This is nonsense. The creation of the Accessory Mechanism not only delivers on the removal of Article of Clothing 15, it allows continued access to the tie for Mary Hopkin, Cilla Black and Peter & Gordon. This is a good deal for Beatles.

Juggling our recording commitments with these negotiations has been difficult. But six years on from that fateful audition, it's now time to get on with the delivery of Rubber Soul. Thank you.

[42]

Our 1992 keynote speaker is someone who needs no introduction, having been at the forefront of the entertainment industry for over thirty years: GEORGE HARRISON.

As a twenty-year-old guitarist in a small-time band, George had no idea where his life was going…until a make-or-break meeting placed success within his grasp.

'I Don't Like Your Tie™ – The Power To Dare' is a once-in-a-lifetime chance to gain business smarts at first-hand from a man whose nerves of steel catapulted his band into the big time.

In this keynote, George will share personal testimony on the importance of audacity in the business environment, promising to give every attendee the power to look any CEO in the eye and say I Don't Like Your Tie™

'I Want To Tell You'…how to leverage the power of I Don't Like Your Tie™ and release the business hotshot 'Within You (Without You)'!
- George Harrison

Tickets: $200 patrons, $350 affiliated, $400 general admission.

[43]

PAUL: Once we'd finished playing we went up to the control room. So we're up there and this is when we meet George Martin for the first time. We all say hello, then he gets down to it - y'know, our equipment, our songs, all that. Which I thought was fair enough.

After all this he asks us if there's anything we don't. And George, bless him, he says 'Yeah, I don't like your tie.' There was a bit of a silence at this so I say to George, trying to smooth things over, 'Don't worry, he can change that.'

But then - I'll never forget this - John jumps in: 'He won't you know, that's the best thing on 'im!' And that encapsulates, for me, the partnership between me and John.

We all laughed, and got back to the discussion - George Martin was saying he'd be able to EQ out some of the amp hiss on Love Me Do. But then John said 'You won't you know, that's the best thing on it!' That was a little strange, but we smiled.

A bit later we stopped for a snack and Norman Smith said he was going to take the tomato out of his sandwich because he didn't like it. John said 'You won't you know, that's the best thing in it!' We weren't really laughing now.

I think he went on to say it about 30 times that evening.

In the end George Martin threatened to eject him from the studio. John said 'You won't you know, I'm the best thing in it,' and the session kind of fell apart. That was John though, y'know? Lovely guy.

[44]

Harrison said nothing.

The man in front of him looked older than his years. Tall. Refined. He'd seen service, that was for sure. Growing up on military bases across Europe in the '50s Harrison had developed a knack of spotting Brits who had done their duty. Sure some looked like professors, but Navy was Navy. Underestimate those guys? Your funeral.

'So,' said the tall man 'I've laid into you for quite a while. Is there anything you don't like?'

There's a moment in every negotiation when it could go either way. And it's in these moments that you find out if the guy by your side is running for the door or staying put.Harrison knew the guys next to him were the latter. From left to right, there was McCartney. Small, a leader, ex-SAS - which was enough information for Harrison. Best, who had once sat motionless for 15 hours during a rehearsal gone bad in Huyton - and John. Thin as a rake but with a streak of crazy wide enough to land a Hercules on. Harrison knew his team inside out. Might as well test the waters.

'I don't like your tie.'

The tall man did not smile. In that moment, Harrison knew. Things were about to head south. And fast. He braced himself, ready to push off from the mixing desk – 6 ft 5in and 250 pounds of hard Liverpool muscle spearheaded by an elbow torquing its way to the left temple. Simple physics. A little geometry. Game over.

'Funny,' said the tall man. 'I'm something of an expert in comedy. I find that people often resort to it when they're nervous. Are you nervous, Mr Harrison?'

'I'm not really the nervous type.'

'Maybe you should be,' said the man, unbuttoning his jacket and revealing an Enfield No.2 Mk I. British issue. An efficient weapon.

'Listen,' said the tall man, beckoning Harrison closer, aiming the pistol at his head. 'Do you want to know a secret?'

John grinned.

George Harrison #24 '*DIE FOR A SHADOW*' by Lee Child.

[45]

Once I heard I'd been cast as George Martin in *Birth of the Beatles* I did a lot of preparation. I read his book, which had just come out I think, and was even lucky enough to meet him in person at an awards ceremony. In the run-up to the shoot I liaised closely with the costume department; the suit they'd got me was fine, but the tie wasn't right at all. It just didn't feel like the kind of tie my 'George Martin' would wear. After a lot of back-and-forth I ended up going out and finding a tie myself – I looked for days until I ended up in some department store just off Regent Street and one particular tie 'spoke' to me, as it were. Once I put it on I really felt like I *was* George Martin. When filming started I only met the actors playing The Beatles a couple of minutes before we started shooting our scene together, so we were able to use that 'getting-to-know-you' feeling and slight uncertainty in our actual performances. Anyway, we played the scene, the director called 'cut' and we waited around while they checked the light and so on. I looked over at 'The Beatles', all of them pretty much unknowns at the time, and said 'That ok? Anything you don't like?' And the actor playing George Harrison, John Altman, says 'Yeah, I don't like your tie.' I must admit, my first reaction to this was anger – who did this nobody think he was? I'd just played the lead in Nicholas Nickleby on

45

BBC One, for goodness sake! But after a moment I saw the funny side of John's remark and always took an interest in his career after that. As a matter of fact it was me that recommended him for the role of Nick Cotton in EastEnders.

Nigel Havers, *My Life On Screen*, Methuen, 2007

[46]

RINGO: I mean the four of us aren't on the best of terms at the minute, as everyone knows. The thing is, each of us at one point or another felt like the other three were really close and he was the odd one out. I know I did – that's why I left in '68; this feeling that I'd been the last one to join the band and they had things which I hadn't been there for – memories, experiences, jokes. When we split conversations got more difficult, and you can't really say to your lawyer: '*Hey can you ask them what that tie thing was all about?*' The next five, six years were rough – it was pretty much drink and thinking about the tie.

So I had this brainwave. Someone told me that Jimmy Nicol was planning to attend a classic car show in Oxfordshire and I thought – hey – this guy was around for a while in the early days. Could he have heard something? So I went. Put a big hat on, turned up my collar and spotted him by an Austin 7. I whipped off the hat. 'Jimmy, we've never spoken, help a drummer out, do you know anything about this tie thing?'

Jimmy just mumbled, 'No... sorry.' He was all fidgety saying he was meeting his friend. I was raving now, I HAD TO KNOW. But his eyes darted to the friend who was arriving with two teas. It was Pete Best. Jimmy said: 'Er... Pete, do you know anything about this tie thing?' Pete was too shocked to say anything.

46

Jimmy was shocked. I was shocked. Three Beatle drummers at a classic car rally. Then it hit me, these guys... they had a lot to talk about. It was tough for them. And here was me, another bloody guy asking them another bloody question about the bloody Beatles.

I left them to it. I was so embarrassed, I bought the Austin 7.

Interview on set of Sextette, 13th December 1976

[47]

Radio 4 Thought for the Day, 12th August 1986

Then George Harrison took a long look at George and said 'Yeah, I don't like your tie!' There was a pause, then George burst out laughing.

For months after that fateful day I pondered upon that incident – it had struck a chord deep within me. Little did I know it but that was the first step on the path which brought me to God.

Because aren't we all in a way standing before Our Lord and saying 'I don't like your tie'? We may not say this in so many words of course, but that remark captures the essence of something very real, very moving and, I think, very human. Which of us has not at some point felt the urge to cry out in pain and bewilderment 'Lord, I don't like your tie!' We feel in that moment that our redeemer has forgotten us, that we are alone in the world and, as we say those words, we truly do not like His tie.

But Our Lord is so rich in love for us that no amount of criticism of His tie will affect the bounteous accessories of his love for us. We can criticise His tie with all our rage and tears and, when we are spent, He will pick us up, encircle us in His perfect wardrobe and, metaphorically speaking, shepherd our

76

careers through a string of number one hits and wildly popular yet also critically acclaimed albums.

As we think upon our own journeys through life, let us remember Proverbs, Chapter 3, Verse 3: 'Never let loyalty and faithfulness leave you. Tie them around your neck.' Amen.

SUE MACGREGOR: That was the Revd Norman Smith with Thought for the Day.

[48]

POPBITCH

No. 396 June 1962

» All tied up «
Which Fab has it in the neck for GM?

We've always thought his productions were absolute comedy but EMI's ex-Fleet Air Arm man George Martin is definitely moving on from twiddling knobs for Peter Sellers and Bernard Cribbins.

It all got a bit heated at a recent audition with everyone's favourite chippy scousers The Beatles. And for once the drama wasn't coming from edgy occasional toilet-seat-wearer John Lennon – who definitely does NOT still live with his auntie, by the way.

It seems a particularly quiet member of the band found his new boss's tie a bit loud – and made his feelings perfectly clear. Cue an awkward silence and a possible 'over before it even began' situation for the band's recording career.

Meanwhile, another band member has been telling all and sundry he 'couldn't even *see* the tie'. Just own up John, nothing wrong with wearing glasses.

48

We've been hearing whispers lately that a certain member of Rory Storm and the Hurricanes may be having a 'the grass is always greener' moment. Surely he'd be Starkey-staring mad to quit...

» Big Questions «
Who's asking what this week?

Which 'stormy' singer is said by those in the know to be up to no good with a certain redheaded cloakroom attendant?

Thanks to: NS, sue_cement_mixer, RMcF, anonx2

Post stories to us: 47 The Mews, Clacton on Sea CO15 1AA. Telegram: CLAC0115

[49]

GEOFF EMERICK: After the split the boys were plagued by people who just wanted them to re-create past glories. It was the same for George Martin. After the band broke up he worked with some of the biggest names in pop, but they all wanted him to do 'the tie thing'.

I continued to work with George at AIR once he got that up and running. At the end of each getting-to-know-you chat the bands would sort of sit there expectantly. At first we wondered what was going on, then at some point George realised they were waiting for him to say 'You've heard quite a lot from me. Anything you don't like?' Then they'd jump in with 'Yeah, I don't like your tie!' They all did it, Stackridge, Cheap Trick, Celine Dion. She was particularly insistent - pointing at his neck and saying 'Well? EH??'

It started to cause a bit of a problem for George as not being on staff at EMI he'd stopped wearing ties every day. So he'd have to remember to put one on whenever a new act came in. That was George to a tee; the perfect gentleman. I'll never forget him sitting there in the control room on Montserrat, no air-con back then; must have been ninety in the shade, sweltering in a full suit just so he wouldn't disappoint Ultravox.

[50]

Then, with immaculate timing, Georgina Harrison pipes up...

'I don't like your necklace.'

Now the thing about Georgina Martin was she had that matrician air about her. Wren at the end of the war, hence the radio background, rose through the ranks at EMI under Olive Preuss – quite old school. And she's falling about laughing!

That was the thing about the girls - they always kept the right side of cheeky. Jane had her edgy wit, Paula was the cute one and Petra Best was just – *film star* gorgeous. Georgina was the quiet one, but make no mistake there was a bit of steel in there.

Who's to say her little gag didn't nudge Georgina Martin into signing them? And that moment gives us all those classic songs. I Saw Him Standing There. A Day In The Life. He's Leaving Home. My favourite? I've a real soft spot for Father Nature's Daughter. So lovely.

Of course, I was in the right place to witness the changes in them over the years – discovering pot in the mid-sixties, then going psychedelic with Strawberry Fields and so on, before the slow fracturing process that led to their break-up.

Of course after that first meeting Georgina Martin did insist on one change. That was really tough for Petra Best. But who can imagine The Beatles without Ringo? Big step putting a bloke in a rock 'n' roll group in those days, but they were trailblazers.

Norma Smith: *Sound On Sound*, **May 1987**

[51]

GEORGE MARTIN: The day had started its downward trajectory at lunchtime to be honest. I was in the canteen having liver and onions which was usually a highlight of the week but this time something about it had changed. The gravy was so...watery, it didn't stick to the liver like it used to. Quite a lot of it ended up dripping down my tie in fact. It was a really nice tie, one I'd only just bought. I took it off and put it in the bin – I'm no expert on cleaning but that much gravy on a silk tie? Not a chance. So that already had me in a bit of a mood. Things threatened to look up briefly in the afternoon when The Beatles came in – I left it to Norman and Ron at first, then Chris Neal came to fetch me to hear this harmonica song which was fairly striking. But then after the session I'm sitting up in the control box with them and at the end when I say 'Anything you don't like?' George Harrison says 'Well for starters...' then he pauses, like he's surveying me, 'I don't like your shirt.' I was pretty bewildered. It was literally just a white shirt. There's a pause. He looks a bit flustered. 'I don't like your...hair?' This really was too much. I mean, criticise people's clothes if you must, but having a pop at someone's physical appearance? That's just not on. Luckily Paul leapt in and smoothed things over – we got on pretty well from that point. The whole experience did put me off George though, and when he brought songs into the studio in the coming couple of years I always made sure we 'didn't have time' to record them, and after a while he gave up. They never sorted out the gravy in the canteen and after a while I stopped going down there.

[52]

Crouched in the tie rack at Liberty's, George did a swift mental re-cap of the situation. Original Timeline George was still at the controls in Friar Park. Evil George from Alternate 1995 Timeline was waiting on the corner of Allerton Road and Church Road on July 6th 1957, ready to stop Ivan and Paul from getting to Woolton Church Fete. Timeline Three George was squashed in George Martin's wardrobe on the morning of 6th June 1962, desperately trying to prevent Timeline Five Evil George from Universe Two destroying the tie. He looked at his ChronoScreen. In forty five seconds George Martin would be approaching the tie rack. George shoved all the other ties onto the floor, leaving only the horse patterned one. Suddenly a trace future-memory hit him, of Timeline12.2 Evil George in the early Bronze Age, trying to thwart the domestication of *equus caballus* then taking the wormhole to London 1874 to run over the future founder of Liberty's in an omnibus. However, he knew as long as Timeline Seven George v2 managed to keep Timeline Four Evil George overpowered on the fire escape outside EMI Studio Two on the evening of 6th June 1962, history would take its intended course. He tensed; George Martin was approaching the tie rack. This was it. This would set everything right.

At that exact moment a towering silver figure appeared behind George Martin, a knife clamped between its metal teeth...Mecha-Ringo.

[53]

'Yoooo hoop!' cried Harrison. 'Leggo of my ear McCartney you rotter!'

His nasal cry echoed up the Remove passage and let it be known to all that Macca of the Fifth had a short way with little ticks like Harrison.

'Shan't!' said McCartney. 'What's all this, y'know, bout you being beastly to Mr Martin? And where's my cake?'

Best and Squinty Lennon popped their heads around the form room door.

'Are you gonna give him what for, McCartney?' the latter chuckled.

'Stay out of it Lennon!' McCartney thundered. 'Or I'll bundle you too! This reedy-voiced villain has scuppered our contract chances - and he's snooped my cake!'

'Yaroooo! It wasn't me!' sobbed Harrison, rubbing an enfattened ear.

'All I said was that Beaky Martin had a stinker of a tie! And the horrid little sound engineer has blabbed the whole thing! Yaaaaaaah - leggo!'

'I'll box you for this Harrison!' said McCartney, unaware of the fact that Best had crouched low behind his ankles. Dancing nimbly into the fray, Lennon yanked down on McCartney's blazer like an overzealous verger given free rein on the church bell.

'Yaaaarrrooo...y'know!' ejaculated McCartney, two thumbs flailing as he toppled backwards onto the newly polished stairs... right into the path of Mr Martin!

'What's this?!' he thundered in a voice resembling that of Stentor of ancient times. 'Sprawling before members of the Remove, McCartney? And you a bass player of the Fifth Form!'

'But... I...' spluttered McCartney. 'I.. Irrghghhhh.'

'Come on, Harrison!' sniggered Lennon, eager to beat a retreat. 'Let's go and finish that cake!'

Harrison Baits the Beak, **Frank Richards, Magnet 1932**

[54]

WENNER: So that period was the start of...

ONO: [inaudible]...really started to come out then. So...

LENNON: Hmm. Mmm.

WENNER: ...when you first really made contact with George Martin, who...

LENNON: I mean there you have it again. George Martin, he's another one of these who've ridden on the Beatles coattails. They still do ride on 'em, you know? [LAUGHS]

ONO: It's true. Only last week ...

LENNON: First time we met him, we'd traipsed down there on bloody new year's day or something I think it was and run through must've been thirty bloody songs in this freezing cold studio. Til There Was You and all that crap that Paul used to make us play. I got a few of what I'd call 'my' ones in there y'know, Money and so on...

WENNER: So do you remember...what were your first impressions of George Martin?

LENNON: The main thing I remember, the only thing I remember as a matter of fact is we were sitting up in his office after we'd finished playing and he just started laying into us. Like an animal, he was. I was shocked – I'd say we all were, you'd have to ask the others.

ONO: It's really hard when...

LENNON: And as usual none of them said anything, just looked down at their shoes y'know? In the end he sort of runs out of steam. Looks at us and says 'And what about you Beatles – anything you don't like?' And I thought bugger this and I looked right at him and said 'Yeah - I don't like your fuckin' tie.'

WENNER: Wow. That's so cool.

***Rolling Stone*, January 1971**

[55]

GEORGE MARTIN: So then George said 'Yeah. I don't like your tie.' I laughed at the sheer cheek of it of course. But even in that moment I was thinking 'This is just what I need.' You see, I could never quite make my mind up about clothes. There was a pressure to fit in... not just the class thing, but I worked with fashionable people; showbiz types.

As I got to know him better I started sounding George out about a few things, a pocket handkerchief here, a waistcoat there, and his judgements were always...he just *knew*.

As The Beatles' career developed so did our partnership – I knew I could send George a simple telegram 'MUSTARD CORDS?' and get a decision.

Then – George came up with a proposal. He wanted me to be a kind of 'guinea pig' for adventurous outfits he was considering. He needed someone he trusted completely, and I felt I 'owed' him rather. His stylist sourced two of everything – one for him, one for me. George would observe me around the studio in say... the furry boots from Let It Be, the pink striped suit, or an enormous flapping bow tie, then decide if it was for him. I was always careful to change back into white shirt and tie if there was a photographer around, and when I left the building.

Of course, as 1969 turned into 1970 and the boys went their separate ways, our little arrangement came to an end. I didn't feel able to turn to George for advice any more, and he couldn't test his new outfits out on me.

Did it affect his choices? That's not for me to say. All I know is that a few months later he's on the cover of All Things Must Pass looking like he'd sourced his clothes from a farmer's bin.

[56]

Not everyone gets on with me fine You don't have to like me - I don't have to like you :)

But people reveal a lot about themselves when they fall back on h8. Do I go around saying 'I don't like your neck'? no. coz I'm not a nob

Yeah yeah 'It was just a joke...' BORING...

I like jokes. But there's a word for a joke at someone else's expense – everyone standing around laughing at you and you don't know where to look...

Bullying : (: (

I've grown + I've a message FOR ALL OF YOUUUUU. I'm a proud, independent, 1950s Rayon tie hanging here in Hard Rock Café Sarajevo, saying 'You will not define me.'

Because THIS tie, is living their best life – and the sad men (it's nearly always men) who go on about this boring old shit on 'Twitter' clearly AREN'T

:)

I'm living loving and LAUGHING. I'm a funny tie! BYE BYEEEEE

PS I watched George's Concert for Bangladesh the other day and thought he looked really smart... KNOT!!!! ¯_(ツ)_/¯

[57]

Once you see the pattern – you can't un-see it. Let's look at the word...TIE.

T is the 19th[th] letter of the alphabet. I, the ninth. And E is the fifth.

1995.

Can it be a coincidence that this was the year that Free as a Bird was released? George, somehow, is very clearly telling us – he did not like this song. And what a surprise! We now find that he wasn't a fan of Now and Then! DESPITE WHAT APPLE'S RETCONNING WOULD HAVE YOU BELIEVE. So let's look at that title...

'NOW AND THEN.' Ten letters. If we divide '1995' by 10. Then Multiply it by 10... guess what?

1995. IT ALL FITS.

Make this point on any Beatles message board, you get laughed at.

Post a perfectly legible dossier to Mark Lewisohn's cousin with EXPRESS INSTRUCTIONS it is to be forwarded to him – you get ignored. EVEN WHEN you've included FOUR FIRST CLASS STAMPS.

Beatles fans are ASLEEP. We need to WAKE UP to what is happening here – stop getting mired in petty irrelevances like

'This wasn't a stereo recording'…'That was an overdub'…'T isn't the 19th letter of the alphabet.'

Now… I turn to a section I call *'Lovecraft Me Do: Lennon, McCartney and Cthulhu.'*

TRANSCRIPT EXTRACT – Jonty Parsons: JBEAT4748864 Live Twitch Stream 24/6/23

[58]

FOR IMMEDIATE RELEASE: Merseybeat Accessory Collection and new Harrison Bequest LIPA.
Mount Street, Liverpool

Here at the Liverpool Institute of Performing Accessories we've always been grateful for the continued support of the Harrison Estate.

From cufflinks worn by Rory Storm at The Majestic Ballroom in Crewe, to monogrammed socks worn by The Tommy Parbold Four, George was always a staunch supporter of LIPA's mission to preserve the Merseybeat accessories which defined this early '60s explosion of Liverpudlian creativity for posterity.

Now a new ***Harrison Bequest*** will inspire a new generation by allowing young musicians to access George's remarkable late '60s wardrobe as seen in Peter Jackson's Get Back.

Whether it's sullen electro-popsters from Wavertree or angular riffing 16-year-old Fall fans with their first support slot at Camp and Furnace – new bands will get the chance to evoke George's unique sartorial flair. From his turtleneck mustard sweater to a simple, very large, black bow tie, nothing is off the table – or left in the wardrobe!

Rapper B97 from Toxteth-based drill outfit Resus said: 'Normally it's just hoods and loose stuff. I didn't think this was for us, but now I've gigged in George's handmade pastel pink striped suit... I do kind of get it.'

Institute Principal Geoff Aspern commented: 'It's great to be able to announce this new Harrison Bequest. It's a living exhibit to add to the wonderful accessories worn by the likes of The Searchers, The Tommy Parbold Four, and The Swinging Blue Jeans.

'I have such fond memories of George visiting us in 1998 – seeing the Merseybeat accessory collection of course inspired him to acquire George Martin's original tie and donate it to us, inaugurating an annual lecture during which a different element of the tie's shortcomings is addressed. It's always a great occasion.'

[59]

PAM AYRES: Right. You probably know that The Beatles didn't get really, properly famous until 1963 but some of us had had our eyes on them a while before that. I'd heard them on Teenagers' Turn back in March '62 and been just ...bowled over, really. Then I heard from a friend's cousin who worked at EMI that they were coming in for a recording session. So what was I to do? I made my way down to London on the day, hoping to 'catch a glimpse' as they say...

Looking back I understand,
   amid that Beatle clamour
   Paul didn't want to hold my hand,
   and make his world a little... Pammer.

She couldn't know it on the day,
   this would-be Beatle wife
   That the man who asked '*Are you OK?*'
   played keys on 'In My Life'.

'Move it grandad! Out the way!'
 I'd spent a mint to get there.
 And now I learn there was that day
 a slur upon his neckwear.

Did George's joke disturb him?
 Loosen this knot of class?
 Did the ageing tie unnerve him?
 And become a looking glass?

Now? I love George Martin.
 And the reason is because:
 The 'One thing I can tell you is...'
 He asked me how I was.

BBC Archive, Pebble Mill At One, Monday, 12th October 1981

[60]

Iconic fashion brand Liberty is partnering with Apple to bring Fab Four fans the chance to own a piece of history: a replica of George Martin's tie.

Liberty Senior Brand Manager Susan Beale says: 'We at Liberty have long been aware of the pivotal role one of our ties played in the story of the world's biggest band, and now we feel it's finally time to let Beatles fans own a piece of this story.

'We've done extensive research to ensure the tie looks exactly like the one George Harrison took offence to on 6th June 1962, right down to recreating a curved incision near the bottom right taper of the tie. Ken Townsend was able to tell us this occurred when it got caught up in the tape machine while George was producing 'Hole In The Ground' for Bernard Cribbins.'

George Harrison's son Dhani is delighted with the new edition tie, saying: 'I don't recall my dad ever mentioning it.'

NB: The George Martin Tie by Liberty In Association with Apple is not to be confused with the 2015 George Martin Tie by Liberty In Association with Apple. The new tie is also available in a collectors' Five Tie Edition for just £590 with a different polyester mix, personally overseen by Giles Martin.

[61]

[012] YEAH, I DON'T LIKE YOUR TIE *(Harrison)*

Harrison vocal

Delivered: 6th June 1962, Abbey Road 2

Target of Quip: George Martin

This typically mordant piece was one of Harrison's first contributions to the band's repertoire (see also [04] WHAT BRINGS MISTER EPSTEIN HERE? (p24)). Opening with a declarative 'I', followed immediately by a blunt Harrisonian 'don't, the piece is sourly resentful in tone and is typically accusatory. Like so many Harrison quips, YEAH, I DON'T LIKE YOUR TIE has an obstinate quality which renders it gawky beside McCartney's apparent effortlessness and anaemic next to Lennon's conceptual daring.

While effective for the first seven words, the work is let down by a descent into bathos on the closing 'tie'.

This must be viewed as a minor work in the Harrison corpus, overshadowed by later triumphs including [128] THERE'S NO POINT MISTER MARTIN GETTING ALL UPTIGHT and [145] YOU DON'T TALK TO A BEATLE LIKE THAT.

[62]

GEORGE MARTIN: Once they'd finished playing they came up to the control room; it was pretty crowded in there with me, my assistants, Brian Epstein and then the five of them, but they all found space eventually. I can just see them now in fact [LAUGHS], John and Paul at the front, then George behind John, Mark next to him and poor old Pete there at the back. I gave them a bit of a talking to, if I'm honest – I'd not been overly impressed with what I'd heard on the studio floor, and told them so. I felt I ought to have a word about their equipment too, more for their sake than mine as I'd be able to supply them with good quality amplifiers if we ever did any more recording together. They listened in silence, pretty much. I remember one of them, possibly Mark, kept sneezing – funny the things you remember isn't it? I still laugh with him about it now. Anyway, at the end of it all I said 'You've heard a lot from me. Is there anything you don't like?' And George Harrison looked straight at me and said 'Yeah, I don't like your tie.' I fell about at this obviously, and they did too, Paul and John leaning on each other, and George, Mark and Pete in a kind of huddle behind them.

By the time they left I knew, or I certainly had a feeling, that I'd be seeing those five young men again.

George Martin: My Life With The Fab Five, **PBS 1992**

[63]

BBC MEDIA RELEASE

Radio Four's Front Row airs first recording of Harrison tie comments.

Published: 2:00 pm, 4 April 2023

When George Harrison visited Stowe School in April 1963 the Beatle was just ten months on from his iconic George Martin 'I don't like your tie' quip.

Teenager John Bloomfield had wanted to bring a little bit of the resulting tie mania to his Buckingham schoolfriends, so wrote to Beatles manager Brian Epstein asking if their guitarist would come and insult their ties.

Now, Radio 4's flagship Arts programme Front Row has revealed the earliest known recording of Harrison being judgemental about ties – made by the pupil that night.

'It was perfect really,' Mr Bloomfield told Samira Ahmed. 'I knew he was selling out ballrooms having a go at the occasional tie, but standards were slipping and fewer people were wearing them. I think this being a school, it was the first time he was confronted with, God, maybe 300 ties at once?

'I wondered if it would be a problem that all of our ties were effectively the same, but as soon as that first "I don't like your tie" rang out across the hall – something in me changed.

'The literal uniformity of the ties didn't put him off at all. He kept the energy up the whole time, just methodically going along criticising the ties, never missing a beat.

'I knew things would never be the same again.'

[64]

GEORGE HARRISON: So George Martin asks us if there's any-thing we don't like and I say 'Yeah, I don't like your tie'. The thing is though...I absolutely loved his tie. I've always had an eye for fashion, ask any of the others, it was me that got cowboy boots first in Hamburg... the leathers too... I had a bigger quiff than any of them back when quiffs were the thing. So naturally I'm going to pick up on a good silk tie; bright colours, really distinctive horse pattern, you know? All I could think of from then on was how to get it off him somehow. I decided I'd talk the tie down so much that he'd ditch it, then I could get my hands on it. And that's what happened. Every recording session after that, he wore the tie and I went on and on and on at him about how awful it was until after about eight months, I think it was the day we did most of the first album in fact, he said 'Right George – I've had enough of this!', took it off and chucked it in the wastepaper basket. When he went to the toilet I got it out and stuffed it in my pocket. I actually wore it to his birthday party that year, but I don't think he noticed. He didn't let on, at any rate. And as you can see, I'm wearing it now. Nice, eh?

[65]

GEORGE MARTIN: So once they'd finished playing we met up in the control room. I remember John and Paul sat on a matchbox on the mixing console, while George and Pete made themselves comfortable on the edge of Norman's glasses case.

Once they were settled I'm afraid I gave them a bit of a talking to. I told them their little instruments weren't up to scratch – I mean, you can make a guitar out of a cotton reel and a couple of matchsticks, but it's never going to sound really first rate. They didn't really react, just smoked their tiny cigarettes and I think John and Paul shared a biscuit crumb they'd found on the console.

At the end I said 'You've heard a lot from me; is there anything you don't like?'

George climbed down from the glasses case onto the console, lowered a length of magnetic tape to the floor and slid down it before making his way across the floor and scrambling up the side of my shoe.

From there he started to climb with remarkable agility, first up the outside of my trousers and then my shirtfront. Once he got to my tie the going seemed to get much harder. It must have been the smoothness of the silk threads, or perhaps he was just tired by this point, but he kept advancing a few inches, then slipping back down - there was one terrible moment when it looked as if he was going to fall – I remember we all gasped, but he recovered himself, thankfully.

In the end I took pity on the poor fellow, picked him up by the back of his jacket and set him on my shoulder. From there, he edged along until his head was pretty much inside my ear, and said 'Well for starters I don't like your tie.'

[66]

GEORGE MARTIN: I said to them 'You've heard quite a lot from me – is there anything you don't like?' George opened his mouth but The Amazing Alexandro started pulling the flags of all nations out of it. I had, in all honesty, wondered why The Beatles had a conjurer in their line-up, but one didn't like to say anything. Once the flags were all out of George's mouth and The Amazing Alexandro had taken a bow while we all applauded, George said 'Well for starters...' but The Amazing Alexandro interrupted him, asking if any gentleman present had a wristwatch. I said I did, so he took it off me and put it in a green velvet bag, which he put on the mixing console before hitting it with a hammer. I was pretty put out at this, but after a bit of business with some rusty cogs and springs The Amazing Alexandro produced my watch, completely intact. Once we'd all applauded again I turned to George and said 'You were saying?' He started speaking again but it was hard to pay attention because The Amazing Alexandro was sawing Brian Epstein in half. It was pretty impressive to be fair, but once he was finished I asked Norman to give him a tour of the studio floor, just to get him out of the way really. Finally George had his chance. 'Well for starters' he said 'I don't like your tie.' Then he looked at me strangely. I looked down at my shirtfront.

66

My tie, which I'd been wearing at the start of the session, was quite gone. I looked down through the control room window to the studio floor and saw The Amazing Alexandro pulling a rabbit out of a hat. It was wearing my tie.

[67]

Something in the tie he wears
  Repels me like it was no other
  Something in the way he knots it,
  It's making me heave a bit,
  I think it looks really shit.

Somewhere in his wardrobe there's
  That tie that I don't want to ponder.
  What a bloody awful purchase.
  I think I need half a sec'
  It shouldn't be round your neck.

I'm asking you will this tie go?
  You don't know, you don't know.
  Was it a bet? Is it for show?
  I don't know, I don't know.

67

Something Mr Martin knows
   That all I have to do is think of it,
   Hanging there above your belt line
   It's making me retch and how
   Please can you remove it now?

George Harrison, 1968

[68]

HOWARD GOODALL: Many people quite rightly see George Harrison telling George Martin he didn't like his tie as a key moment in the band's early story. What fewer people know is that George's comment is part of an illustrious lineage of cheeky-yet-endearing remarks between artist and prospective patron. Mozart, for example, when first brought in to the presence of Emperor Joseph II in 1781 charmed the notoriously chilly monarch by telling him he didn't like his wig, thereby earning himself a royal patronage which lasted many years. Going even further back we are reminded of a surviving extract from the diary of Leopold, Prince of Anhalt-Köthen. In June 1717 he writes 'After morning chapel I met with a man applying himself for position of Kapellmeister.

'Being beset by my familiar ague I sought to ensure our interview was conducted with brevity but the fellow made great sport, telling me he did not like my breeches. This amused me greatly and I told Herr Bach he could take up the post as of Lammastide.' Moving back to the twentieth century it is entirely possible that George Harrison was among those watching when young composer Malcolm Arnold told the then-82-year-old Ralph Vaughan Williams that he didn't like his belt during an appearance on In Town Tonight on October 2nd 1954.

68

And the phenomenon continues into the modern era; earlier this year audiences gasped during King Charles's coronation concert as Katy Perry told the new king she didn't like his crown. Of course, true to tradition the monarch saw the funny side and rewarded Perry by appointing her Chancellor of the Duchy of Lancaster.

[69]

GEORGE MARTIN: So when they'd finished these four young chaps came up to see me – I'd been watching them on and off for the past couple of hours and thought they just might have what it took to succeed in this industry, but I wanted to have a chat with them before making any decisions. Once they'd all sat down I told them a bit about my role as chief designer at the tie factory, about our organisation's place in the UK neckwear industry, that kind of thing. Then I'm afraid I gave them a bit of a talking to; I said their designs for new ties were nothing special, the trial ties they'd made that evening were pretty poor and while there was obviously something appealing about them I still wasn't sure they had what it took to make it as tie designers. Once I'd finished they all just looked at me. I said 'Is there anything you don't like?' Then George Harrison piped up 'Yeah, I don't like your record'. I had a Dansette in my office and used to play all the latest hits while I designed ties. At that moment it was playing 'How Do You Do It?' by The Tommy Parbold Four, which was number one at the time. I had to pause a moment to process what George had said but in the end I just burst out laughing at his cheek. And that was the start of almost a decade of tie-making with the boys – we went on to make a string of ties which really changed people's notion of what a tie could be. My favourite? I was very fond of 'the white tie', as it became known. But I did always feel it should have been about half the length.

[70]

'Yeah, I don't like your tie.'

A silence filled the air.

The old otter leaned back on his tree stump, shaking a few stray drops of river water from his hind legs. His keen, intelligent eyes stared back at the youngster, whose whiskers twitched apprehensively.

He looked at the other three – one uneasily twitching his hairless tail, one nervously eating an acorn held in both paws; the one at the back so frightened he had curled up into a ball with only his spiky spines showing.

The otter bared his teeth slightly at the other animals. They shivered with fear, but the snarl turned into a smile, then a grin, then a silent, wheezing chuckle. Soon he was rolling on his back, laughing for all he was worth.

One by one the other animals joined in. They rolled on the floor, kicked their little feet up in the air and laughed until they were limp.

Before long the otter had got in touch with the little animals' water vole manager and arranged a follow-up session, leading to a years-long streak of record-breaking acorn collecting.

As the years wore on, some woodland creatures noted that the otter rarely seemed to give as much attention to the little rabbit's acorn collection as he did to the acorns the water-rat and the squirrel collected together. Within six summers the little rabbit believed his acorn collections were every bit the equal of his two bigger friends but his efforts were still relegated to the end of acorn-gathering sessions.

When the animals eventually went their own ways the little rabbit had, for a while, the greatest success at acorn collecting and was loved throughout the forest. As time went on however his one-time bandmates' own solo acorn collection careers began to flourish and he was once again overshadowed. It was but small comfort to him when in 1987 the old otter told Q Magazine 'I always felt rather sorry for neglecting him.'

[71]

MAGIC ALEX: I had not been at Apple long when George Martin approached me. I went with the boys to the studio one day and during a break he said he wanted to ask me a question. Ever since his first encounter with George Harrison he had been bothered that something he had worn had upset someone; it played on his mind. He told me he had an idea; a tie which detected the tastes of the person looking at it and changed its appearance to suit them, and wondered if I could develop a prototype - a tie impossible to dislike. I got to work, and in a couple of weeks it was done. I took the tie to George myself – they were all in the studio that day, working on what became known as The White Album. George was delighted – he put the tie on straight away. The boys all took turns looking at the tie and telling us what they saw – for John it was pure white, Paul saw a swirling mass of colours, for Ringo it was red and white stripes and George Harrison said it had 'a kind of sunrise glow'. Then George Martin looked down at the tie himself and I realised that I had forgotten to tell him – the person wearing this tie must not look at the tie while wearing it, or the tie will...it is difficult to explain. The tie will ...look back at them. George Martin stared for a moment, then started wailing and ran out of the studio. He was gone for over two weeks. The story since then has been that he was on holiday, but he was not. While he was away George Harrison destroyed the tie and burned its remains. He did not speak to me for weeks.

[72]

GEORGE MARTIN: ...so they all trooped upstairs and made themselves comfortable in the control room. Once they were all settled I'm afraid I rather laid into them. I remember pretty clearly saying 'Your playing, your repertoire, your equipment; all first rate. No problems there. The real issue is your ties.' They were all wearing identical black ties, to go with their suits. I looked at John first; his was in a particularly poor state. I don't know if he'd been chewing it or something but the end was an absolute mess. 'You'll get nowhere with a tie like that.' I remember saying. Then I turned to Paul. 'Didn't anyone show you how to tie a tie properly?' He had a pretty ragged half-Windsor, pulled so tight the knot was about the size of a marble. Their drummer was right at the back but I could still see the pretty sorry specimen around his neck, riddled with cigarette burns. 'That really won't do at all' I said.'

He looked pretty mortified at this – I actually felt rather sorry for him. Then, right at the front, was George. 'And as for you,' I said, 'At least you've made an effort. Clean. Well proportioned. Smart knot. Equal hang at the front and back. That's a really, really lovely tie.' They just sat there in silence. I said 'You've heard a lot from me. Is there anything you don't like?'

Now it takes a particular kind of personality to speak up at a moment like that. To disagree. And at that point, George quite calmly announced that he didn't like his own tie. Amazing guy.

[73]

Those first weeks at Twickenham weren't without their hiccups however – I remember one day things really blew up…

Paul was at the piano running through his Maxwell Edison song for Dick James when George, looked over at him and said 'If Pataphysics is anything at all, it's "the science of imaginary solutions". Why would Joan need a test tube, Paul?'

Ringo started to say something but George rounded on him. They'd always been close, so this was a real surprise.

'Mantel shelf? Mantel SHELF? That's not even a thing, Richy. It's "mantelpiece".'

John tried to stick up for Ringo, but he got both barrels too.

'"Rattle your jewellery"? Rattle your jewellery??? Jewellery doesn't rattle, John.

Not enough to make a sound equivalent to clapping anyway.' I could tell John didn't like this. He fixed George with one of his down-the-nose stares. '"Anything you don't like?" "Yeah I don't like your tie." I'm Beatle George Harrison – quietly sardonic but with a lovable lopsided wit. "I don't like your tie". "I don't like your tie."'

It wasn't long after this that George walked out.

Michael Lindsay-Hogg, *Luck and Circumstance,* **2011**

[74]

BARBARA WALTERS: What do you make of all this new technology in music...record scratching and 'sampling' and all the rest of it?

RINGO: I'm all for it. The Beatles were always up on technology. We'd rush round if someone had a Moog.

In fact, just last year I was in New York, dropping off Paul's broken Yamaha CS-80 with a guy called Harold Cohen. He fixed synths - but he was also working on an 'autonomous drawing program' called AARON. He was in town displaying it at the American Association of Artificial Intelligence.

Harold told me that this program, if you gave it enough information, could create an image for you. Maybe you'd found out that a joke people kept laughing at was about something you'd never seen. You could get people who HAD seen it to offer all the information they could, and AARON would recreate it. Then you wouldn't feel so bloody left out if it came up in future. I did give him a request, yes.

Anyway. Harold had started in C Programming Language and his transition to LISP or LIST Processing only came in the '90s, and we were a long way off the modern hexadecimal numbering and iterative programming algorithms we have now.

So...while AARON looked like it might be able to produce the image...y'know. Not to be.

He fixed the synth though. It's the one Paul used on Wonderful Christmastime.

Barbara Walters (CNN) 31/03/81

[75]

There was a definite pause after George said it. You know, that moment – someone tries a joke and you think... '*ooh there's a bit of bite to that!*'

George Martin went quiet for a moment. Then he shrugged and said: 'Really? Well I don't like your face.'

Harrison nodded, and said: 'Why? Is it a bit like your mum's?'

Quick as a flash, George Martin says: 'No. This tie does remind me of YOUR mum though. Seen better days. Bit worn.'

George smiled at this. 'That's funny because the minute I saw it I thought of your mum. Is she still doing the wrestling?'

'Didn't your mum work near the docks?' Martin replied, pretending to adjust the control desk. 'Nothing to do with the ships, obviously.'

Harrison was lighting a fag now. 'Didn't you have to hire a cargo ship last time your mum visited?'

'We did yes!' laughed George. 'Thirty crewmen. Bet they kept your mum busy.'

John and Paul looked ... mortified. It just went on and on. The whole session was shelved for that day.

But the two Georges went out for dinner. It carried on there for about three hours until the waiter asked them to leave.

Ken Townsend, quoted in Bob Masterson: *Rock's Greatest Insults.* **Chapter Seven 'Beatle Burns'.**

[76]

Stage in darkness but for MOUTH, upstage audience right, about 8' above stage level, faintly lit from close-up and below, rest of face in shadow. Invisible microphone.

VOICE: ... up ... up from this studio ... the control room... no sooner fastened up his collar...his collar his...... brought up as I had been to believe......and now this stream ... words were ... powerless to respond... what? ... who? ... no!... the buzzing? ... yes ... all the time the buzzing...Barcelona... for on that June evening... not catching the half of it......such fervour... fervour... proof if proof were needed... brought up as I had been to ... with the others ... in a merciful ... (brief laugh) ... God ... (good laugh) ... first thought was ... oh long after ... sudden flash... Eldorado... ...what? ... who? ... no! ... he! ... HE! ... (pause) ...I don't like your tie.

A spotlight picks out TIE, upstage audience left about 8' above stage level.

Blackout.

Not Tie, Samuel Beckett, 1963

[77]

Fellow recipient Sir Geoffrey Ponford recalls the day. 'Replete with their MBEs the four of them stood before Her Majesty in their silly suits looking very pleased with themselves. The Queen had taken the trouble to inform them as to how the day would progress, where they could find refreshments, where they would proceed to for the later aspects of the reception, where they might greet the press etc.

'Throughout all of this the little fellow, Harrison I think, was staring at Her Majesty's brooch.

'At this point, The Queen asked The Beatles if, they had enjoyed their day, and if there was anything they didn't like. It was like Harrison was hypnotised. He was just staring at the brooch. He seemed about to say something....

'The McCartney fellow very quickly jumped in, put his hand on Harrison's shoulder and said. "No. No problems at all, Your Majesty. Very good." Lennon seemed to enjoy this.'

77

With the benefit of hindsight, Her Majesty's choice to greet The Beatles wearing the 1846 Valencia Brooch gifted to Queen Victoria by Lord Carfax (who was vocal in his dislike for a growing informality in popular musical performance) seems appropriate.

To Our Century – A Queen. HM Queen Elizabeth II, **Sir Anthony Beldon, Triumph, 1992**

[78]

From: Richard Curtis

Date: Tuesday, 16 May 2022 at 12:18

To: Stacey Benet, Josh Marcombe, Todd Manfield, Jenna Stacey

Subject: RE: New Beatle Project Script recap

Hi Guys

Thanks for all the work on the early outline. Title wise, **YES-TIE-DAY?** Bit shit? **KNOT GUILTY**??

To recap, '60s Liverpool, young George Harrison (TIMOTHÉE CHALOMET???) despairs of his life as an apprentice rock guitarist. Pursues his dream of fashion design. (How good did he look in Get Back btw??) The world is hit by a blackout, and George is hit by a bus (can someone check 1962 Liverpool bus timetables?) He wakes to find all the ties have disappeared and NO ONE REMEMBERS THEM. Bit of a stretch but bear with. Taking advantage of his knowledge, George 'invents' the tie, and his hailed as a fashion genius across the globe.

78

The ties get better and better, increasingly experimental -- story story story, success proves hollow as he realises the thing that really matters to him is his girlfriend Patti. Possible love triangle here?

This draft mentions a 'climatic' scene at The Global Tie Convention, not sure what this has to do with the weather -- can we keep an eye on that? George learns what he really values etc etc.

Heart of the film is in a poignant scene, George visits the fashion legend and tie supremo Jacques Montcrieff, who in this reality, did not asphyxiate due to an overly tight Windsor knot.

Older, wiser, George opts for the simple life of a rock guitarist, film mogul and populariser of Eastern spirituality in the West.

Great! Now. Big question Do you think we can get the rights to the ties?

[79]

BILLY J KRAMER: There were great benefits to sharing management with The Beatles. I mean, how many other singers had their first three singles written for them by Lennon and McCartney? But the real gift was getting George to write your enigmatic but cheeky one-liners. When Brian heard what George said to George Martin about his tie he saw the potential straight away – George was an enigmatic but cheeky one liner *machine.* So Brian said he'd get George to write me some. I'll always remember one week in June '63 I think it was – I got a package from NEMS. In it was an acetate of Bad To Me and a piece of paper in George's handwriting with about twenty one-liners on it. I was due to do my first interview that week, with Record Mirror, and thought I'd try one of them out. So when the journalist said to me 'What are your long-term ambitions Billy?' I looked down at the list I'd got from George and picked one. 'I'm not big enough for long-term ambitions yet. I'm still in short-term ambitions.' It got a big laugh, looked great in print and really helped me. The problem was, Lennon and McCartney were finding it very hard to get their cheeky one-liners picked up. They could look a bit sullen. Resentful. Of course before long I started thinking it was me, not George's quips, which was winning everyone over, so I told Brian I'd be writing my own opening lines from now on, thank you very much. And of course we all know how that went. I came to my senses in it must have been '68 and went back to George, cap in hand. But he was writing sardonic quips for Badfinger by then and I never heard back from him.

[80]

NORMAN SMITH: After the session they came up to the control room for a chat with George. He really did lay into them; their songs, their equipment, their playing, all the time with his dæmon, this great big eagle, sitting on the mixing desk. I can picture the four of them now as they listened; John with his hedgehog dæmon, Paul with his leopard, Pete with his newt and George Harrison with his ermine. At the end of George's spiel he said to them: 'You've heard quite a lot from me – anything you don't like?' There was silence. John's hedgehog curled up into a spiny ball, Paul's leopard arched its back and scratched at the studio carpet. Then, George Harrison's dæmon scuttled over and jumped up on the desk where George Martin's was, went up on its hind legs and whispered something. There was a pause as the eagle took in whatever it was the ermine had said, and for one awful moment I thought it was going to rip the poor thing to shreds, but after a second it bent its head and rubbed the side of the ermine's neck with its beak. We all relaxed at this and things were much easier after that. Within a few minutes I noticed the eagle had moved off from the ermine and was perched comfortably between the leopard and the hedgehog.

80

The ermine looked a bit sulky at this, like it was going to go home and write a triple album by itself. The last thing I remember as I left was the eagle looking very intently at Pete's newt.

[81]

EXTRACT – **The Abbey Road Mob: My life in EMI by Ronnie Kray.**

It was a surprising comment from Harrison because everyone knew what George Martin, 'the gaffer' we used to call him, was like. But anyways the lad said it and that was that. You reap the whirlwind.

The gaffer kind of slowly stood up. Scratched his chin. I was watching from the desk and just thought 'Christ 'ere we go.' He slowly took Harrison by the lapels, lifted him just a touch and said: *'I beg your pardon?'*

The lad probably got a better view of the gaffer's scar close up. The one Flanders had given him for putting Swann in the hospital. The gaffer had come up with a good racket. You get a group in the studio, one of them has an 'accident', you replace him with one of your own men. The gaffer was known for it. How else d'you think Jack 'The Hat' McVitie ended up in Beyond The Fringe?

Spike Milligan got a bit bolshy about the gaffer's plan to place Tony Lambrianou in his gang. Just would not take it. Not long after, the police discovered the remains of the The Goons in Epping Forest. Very sad. Promising boys.

81

Needless to say that day Harrison had his well-documented accident with the piano lid. So that was that it for him as a guitarist. The gaffer pointed to me and said: 'Ronnie. Congratulations. You're the guitarist in The Beatles. Now learn Besame Mucho or I'll cut ya.'

The funny thing is, being in The Beatles really changed me. For example in India I got heavily into meditation – it was like a whole new level of awareness. But then we had to leave 'cos I done Maharishi with the cosh.

[82]

It was at that point that one of them, George I think, said: 'Yeah. I don't like your tie.'

Well this really took George Martin off guard. He was bent double laughing! After a minute, he had to rear up to try and get some air in his lungs – he was just *roaring*. He was laughing so hard the mics down on the studio floor were picking it up and sending the level meters into the red but the engineers were too busy rolling around to care!

One of them, John maybe, was just delighted with the joke, big smile, limbs everywhere. The bass player's face lit up, shaking his head with a lovely laugh. And the handsome drummer was laughing so hard he literally fell off his chair.

We just couldn't get over how cheeky it was! But so funny too.

We weren't going to get anything more done that evening. George Martin just waved the whole session off, still laughing. Great bunch of lads. I sometimes wonder what happened to them.

Chris Neal, My EMI Diary 1962 – 66. **Spin Wave Books, 2011**

140

[83]

Sexy Sadie session tape, Friday 19 July 1968

Ken Scott: Sorry George, what did you say?

George Harrison: I said it's no point in Mr Martin being uptight.

Paul McCartney: Right, so...

George Harrison: You know, we're all here to do this, and if you want to be uptight...

George Martin: I don't know what to say to you, George.

George Harrison: I mean, you're very negative.

George Martin: [INAUDIBLE] ...coming from you.

Paul McCartney: Er. [LAUGHS] Perhaps we could...

George Harrison: I want to know what he means first.

John Lennon: [SINGING] 'What about Millie Sutcliffe/And her brother Dan?'

George Martin: I was just thinking back to the first time you came in here...

George Harrison: Perhaps if Mr Martin could get over something that happened four years ago and concentrate on the job in in hand...

George Martin: It was from *Liberty*, you know.

Paul McCartney: OK, let's go again. This'll be the one. 1, 2, 3, ...

[84]

CHRIS NEAL: The first couple of songs were nothing special. Once they got to the one with the harmonica Norman must have heard something in them though, cos he sent me down to fetch George Martin. While I was gone the evening tea trolley came round so I missed it.

Of course I'd had to meet their manager in reception and help the other bloke get all the gear in so I'd missed the afternoon break too. I was starving.

Once they'd finished playing George got them up here, taking them to task over God knows what. I wanted to get the paperwork done as quick as I could so I could go and eat.

As I worked I was mentally running through what we had in at home – it was a Wednesday I remember and that's the day Liz does the shopping.

I hoped she'd got pork chops again - last ones we got, from the new butcher by the cinema were really good.

Or perhaps a pie – I could stop off at the pie stall on the way home if I hurried, it's just by the tube, and pick us up a pie each. I was practically fainting just at the thought of it, finishing off the session sheet while George gave those Scousers what for.

As I was crossing the final T's there was a sudden silence, then one of them, the little sulky one, said something and they all fell about laughing. I didn't stick around to hear what it was all about. That pie stall closes at ten.

[85]

NORMAN SMITH: One thing people always mention about being around the Beatles is their charisma, and it's true; from the first time I met them they just radiated a sense of...fun. During that very first session when they were all laughing with George Martin about his tie I thought 'I wish that were me.' So I thought I'd follow George's lead – wear a tie so bad they'd make fun of it and I'd have the same rapport with them as he did. Next day I came into work in the worst tie I owned – one of those horrible thin ones, in a sort of mustard colour. Nothing. I was pretty gutted, I can tell you. Next day I came in in my oldest suit, shirt with the collar missing, and the same tie as the day before, but put on backwards with the label facing out. Not a dickie bird. So over time I stepped it up – string vest and football shorts...wetsuit and an old flying helmet. Not a peep. The final straw came in late '65. They were listening to the playback of Drive My Car, me sat there in full SS uniform, and no one said a word about it. The next day I went to management and asked if I could start running my own sessions. They'd been impressed by my work with The Beatles so they agreed. A while later I was working with The Pink Floyd and they asked if we could go in and meet the boys, who were in the middle of Sgt Pepper. I said yes and at a suitable point we went into Studio Two. The two bands start chatting – quite happily in fact. Just before we leave to get back to the Floyd session, George Harrison comes over to me, looks right at me and says 'What happened to your mustard tie, Norman?'

[86]

"HANCOCK'S HALF HOUR"
SID'S MUSIC STUDIO
No.8 Fifteenth series
with
TONY HANCOCK, SIDNEY JAMES, KENNETH WILLIAMS, BILL KERR
INCIDENTAL MUSIC COMPOSED BY WALLY STOTT AND RECORDED BY THE BBC AUGMENTED REVUE ORCHESTRA
SCRIPT: RAY GALTON & ALAN SIMPSON

SID All right lads gather round. Great day's work that. Sign this contract you get a straight five nicker. All happy? Good.

HANCOCK Hang on a minute! You won't get me that easily. I'm going to get my accountant down at The Hand and Racquet to take a look at this...

SID No time boy, no time. Sign here, I'll hold your harmonica...

BILL Remember Tub, I'm still paying him for the hire of me bass...

HANCOCK Hire of your bass? You buffoon. He SOLD it you two months ago!

SID So. Minus five bob for the use of the pen. Let's see, two nicker for hiring the mics. Two nicker for the mic stands...

HANCOCK Two quid for mic stands?! I'll hold 'em meself for that!

SID ...and a quid for the tape.

HANCOCK This is an outrage! The Remo Four don't have to put up with this. I've seen better recording kit in a skip outside Decca. We're off!

SID Look boy, as your official advisor, courtesy of Sid James Music Production Ltd I officially advise you to sign with The Sid James Music Agency Ltd. Now, is there anything you don't like?

SNIDE I say, your tie don't 'alf look funny!

HANCOCK He's right you know, he's dead right – what a horrible tie. How you can walk about in society Sid with that monstrosity round your neck simply beggars belief. I mean... Hang on a minute...you twister, that's MY TIE!

[87]

NORMAN SMITH: George Martin had been missing for about three weeks before Ken Townsend and I came up with the idea of making a robot replacement. I got hold of a shop dummy and dressed it in some clothes George had left in the studio; Ken called in a favour from a pal at Madame Tussaud's and got one of their spare Duke of Edinburgh heads. Comb the hair differently, keep the control room lights low, job done. I must say it worked like a dream. Ken and myself were more than capable of covering the sessions and whenever top brass wanted to talk to George we had a system rigged up, tape loops of him speaking from old sessions, with buttons we could press to give general answers; 'Yes.' 'No.' 'Your repertoire's not up to much.'

Everything went without a hitch until that night The Beatles came in. By now Ken and I had the whole thing down to a fine art; 'Mr Martin's busy but he hopes to come down later', handle the session ourselves, then give them a three-minute chat with the dummy and its tape loops upstairs. It was all fine, right until the point where we played the 'Anything you don't like?' loop. George Harrison looked straight at the dummy for what felt like an age and I thought 'This is it – we've been rumbled.'

But then he just said something Beatley and they all laughed. Me and Ken breathed a sigh of relief!

Eventually pretty much every engineer at Abbey Road ended up on shifts with a non-disclosure agreement, operating the robot. But it couldn't last. Paul leaned over him at the mixing desk and knocked his head off. They were filming for Anthology at the time so the whole thing was caught on camera. Luckily Paul, George and Ringo agreed by now it was probably best to keep the whole thing quiet, so that's what we agreed to do.

[88]

NORMAN SMITH: After they'd finished playing they came up on deck to talk to George. The waters were a little rough that evening, but nothing too bad. They leaned on the railing while George relaxed against the rigging. He spent a little while going through their equipment and repertoire, telling them both would need to be improved if they were to become successful. During this speech the prevailing south-westerly got the better of us. All four of them looked pretty green around the gills, I can tell you. We used to see that a lot with new acts, many of whom had never been in an ocean-going studio before. Just as George is telling them that Love Me Do is the song with the most promise, John goes absolutely ashen faced, turns round and is sick over the side. Real heaving and groaning stuff. This sets Paul off; he only just makes it to the side before letting loose. George tries to carry on his talk, but by this point the rain's lashing them all too, they can barely hear him. Pete had had his head down pretty much since he arrived so it took me a moment to realise he was being sick on the deck. He looked mortified, the poor fellow. What with the storm and all the vomiting there didn't seem to be much point in carrying on so, yelling above the noise of rain on the port-side.

George asked them if there was anything they didn't like. 'Well, for starters' said George Harrison, and at that point the boat hit an enormous wave, pitched horribly and he was sick all over George's tie. That's why to this day I always conduct a group's first session on an inland waterway, or perhaps a boating lake.

[89]

Audition

Their fathers from an age not made for fun,
Whose wives conspired to give them beatnik sons
Who lived upstairs, and didn't look like them.
They've put their Elvis Presley on again.
And sang like they were yanks and grew their hair
And lurked in basement nightclubs, came home late,
Escaped to London. Left them asking 'Why?'
Mr Martin makes his records there.
The youngest of them as they spooled the tape
Had flatly told him: 'I don't like your tie.'

That night he folds the relic. Combs his hair.
Old comedy recordings. Books. That chair.
Youth is now an echo from afar.
That picture when he joined the Fleet Air Arm.
Maybe that tie's a noose. But he reflects
That those boys really could get round the necks
Of high street Rickenbackers, Hofner bass –
The young one with the pointy shoes. That face.

And as he stumbles, groping, for a piss
Considers if he's really right for this.
He sleeps. And does not know that he will share
Their threefold affirmation:
Yeah, Yeah, Yeah.

Philip Larkin, *Tie Windows* **(1974)**

[90]

That joke of George's summed up The Beatles for us. I wrote about that night in one of the little printed sheets we used to pass round. Moments like that gave you a bit of hope...

Liverpool was right next to Cammell Laird shipyard so they were hit hard as kids. It was a prime target in The Blitz – right through to 1947. The whole country was... exhausted. Operation Sea Lion was what... '49? They just rolled over us. All we knew was the occupation.

By the late '50s The Nazis were a bit stretched. The Americans were staying out of it but the Government In Exile under Churchill were pumping cash in. So you could pull off little resistance gigs.

Band would arrive, quick stage set up, local teenagers would rush out, it was like... a village fete.

John was doing his Hitler thing when the Gestapo arrived. The big man pulled out George in front of everyone. Pistol in hand. Going on about degenerates. The Nazi says: 'I don't like your music.' That's when George said it. Nazis don't like being laughed at. So he raised the gun.

He didn't see Pete Best creeping up behind him from the kit, and in a flash Pete stuck him with his Fairbairn-Sykes. Pete had seen some action in Coventry so he wasn't a man to be messed with. The crowd turned on the Germans and The Beatles lived to play another day.

They were something else. It was a tragedy they never got to record. But I still remember the songs.

Archive testimony, *Britain under the Nazis: 1949 – 1967.* **Chapter 9: The Beat Resistance.** *Professor Jane Randall. Oxford University Press, 1998.*

[91]

ARTHUR KELLY: I've been friends with George since we both started at The Institute. He was pretty much the first person I met there, and we were friends straight away. Even at the age of eleven George stood out. He was wearing school uniform, obviously, but he'd modified bits of it; cap on sideways, huge fat knot in his tie and he'd found some way, God knows how, of making his school trousers look like drainies. All the same, he was good as gold - always first to put his hand up when one of the masters asked a question and all that. Well brought-up boy, our George. One day early on we were out in the yard, still new boys, not really knowing what to do with ourselves. This master comes over, I can see him now – great big feller. Looks down at us and he says 'What do you think you're wearing, Harrison?' and George looks down at the floor and just sort of mumbles 'Don't know, sir.'

And this bloke really lays into him, y'know: 'How dare you come to school looking like that. If you wanted to get your school career off on the wrong foot you're going the right way about it' and all this. George's head is still down and I'm not sure if he's crying. 'And another thing' says the master 'I don't like your tie.' And that was it for George and school. Pretty soon after that he got his first guitar.

[92]

Wednesday June 6th 1977

To Savile Row to film my bit for Eric's NBC thing. A real frisson to be filming a scene mocking Apple right outside Apple's former HQ. George H arrived bang on time, looking wiry and trim. Once he'd been transformed into his reporter character it was wonderful to see people passing him by with not a clue who he was. When we came to our brief scene I did my best Derek Taylor, not an impersonation exactly but I think I captured that louche-yet-slightly-nervy air he has. I'm sure he'll tell me in due course. George did a good job as the earnest reporter, oblivious to all the loot being carried away behind his back. During a break in filming he asked how JC and I cope with people constantly demanding the Dead Parrot sketch, quoting it back at us etc. I told him it's not too bad. It brings people pleasure and on that basis I'm fine with it. I suppose for a restlessly creative, searching mind like George it'd be the stuff of nightmares. Being pinned down to just one joke, having some idiot constantly harping on about one famous line, pulling apart its ramifications with ENDLESS different versions and interpretations. He'd hate it.

92

Lovely meal in the evening. Terry J came round, and Helen did shepherd's pie.

The Python Years: Diaries 1969-79, **Michael Palin. Weidenfeld & Nicholson 2006**

[93]

TOM PETTY: I got the call from George must have been mid '86. He said he was putting together a group and would I be interested? I asked George who else was in it and he said Bob Dylan, Roy Orbison and Jeff Lynne. My jaw just about hit the floor. Dylan and Orbison in the same band? With George Harrison? Wow. I asked George what the idea was and he explained that he'd noticed a lot of people in rock were funny. He'd done his famous tie joke, Dylan had had a big hit with 'What are your songs about?' 'Most of them are about four minutes' and of course people just loved Roy's 'Mercy!' on Pretty Woman. George added that he'd got Jeff Lynne in cos he thought that vocoder voice on Mr Blue Sky was hilarious. He wanted to make an album where he wryly criticised people's neckwear while Dylan told people how long the songs were, Roy went 'Mercy' and Jeff said 'Please turn me over' through his vocoder. I asked what my role would be – I mean I'm not particularly known for my wit, you know? George said he wanted someone who he knew and trusted to hold things together while they all did their bits. I was flattered as hell. So the next day I got my guitar and headed over to Roy's place for the first rehearsal.

93

They were all there when I arrived and before long we got going - them all doing their bits and me on guitar and...it was awful. So I suggested we scrap it and make an album of likable country-tinged rock instead. Worked out pretty well.

[94]

CHRIS NEAL: It's gone down in history, that line about the tie. I never thought it was funny. I'd worked with George Martin for a while by then so seeing his taste in ties mocked like that really got my back up. I decided there and then, 6th June 1962, that I'd get George Harrison for that. I knew it was important to bide my time though, get all my ducks in a row. Five years I waited, until late in 1967 I casually mentioned to an acquaintance whose father worked in the City that Clive Epstein didn't seem to be relishing running NEMS as much as his brother had, and might be looking to sell. Clive turned down Triumph Investment Trust's first approach as we all know, but I told them to give it a year then try again. I didn't spend that year idle; I knew Ian Stewart from the Stones slightly and planted the notion that he talk Mick into recommending John meet with Allen Klein. Meanwhile, Triumph came back to Clive with a second offer, and this time he accepted. This led to the chain of events which ended with the Beatles missing out on the chance to acquire NEMS, taking their eye off the ball with the Northern Songs situation and ultimately losing the rights to their own catalogue. By that point Klein was managing all of them apart from Paul; that caused a massive rift and that was basically it for them.

94

It was a shame for John, Paul and Ringo, but I couldn't let that insult stand. Harrison had to pay. It really was a lovely tie.

[95]

NORMAN SMITH: I suppose now after all these years, I can come clean: the tie thing didn't actually happen. When the Beatles got big people started asking me what it was like meeting them for the first time and the real version was bit boring, so I made something up.

Don't get me wrong, George and the boys had a great rapport, and there were plenty of times where incidents *like* the tie thing happened, just not on that occasion.

In reality they just ran through the songs then came up for a chat and George gave them a bit of a talking to. I'd experienced the same thing – he played hell with me once when my Bugatti blocked his space in the car park!

After they left I remember him saying what nice lads they seemed, but we weren't in stitches like I said we were.

Certainly nothing like as funny as the time I went on holiday to Paris with Sammy Davis Jr.

I think once George and the boys heard my tie story being repeated, they started to think it had actually happened – none of them's ever contradicted it anyway. For a while I was afraid of getting found out, the way I imagine someone who uses a fake CV to get a job in a recording studio might feel, but no-one cottoned on.

95

Like I said, the tie thing's always been on my conscience; I'd hate you to get the impression I just go around making things up. That's completely untrue.

[96]

Wednesday 6th June 1962. Back to work after two days' sick. Didn't really feel well enough to go back but don't want to make waves while I'm still quite new. Plus of course since x and I got together it's not like going into work, not really. Hard though, working at opposite ends of the building; me in the typing pool at the Abbey Road end, x right over the other side in the kitchens. We manage a moment here and there though. Canteen's no good – too many people. Same with Reception. So we hide away. The tape library, that stationery store just down from Sir Joseph's office - we find somewhere to steal a minute or two most days. Together. This evening it was the storeroom just over from Two. Mr Martin had a band in; I'd heard some of their session through the door earlier. x really down. Breaks my heart. Crying. Saying there's no way it can ever work out for us. This set me off too. We just looked at each other. Both thinking 'Is this it?' I was just about to say let's stop then let's just leave it there's nothing either of us can do but just as I opened my mouth there was this burst of laughter from Two's control room. Hearing that sound...I can't explain, but it changed something. I started smiling, then x did too. I can't explain it.

166

96

We'd just been about to end but it suddenly that didn't seem to matter. Just that laughter. We kissed. I think things are going to be all right.

[97]

Yahoo News US 23rd May 2023

Over fifty years since the break-up of The Beatles, it seems Paul McCartney and Ringo Starr are still best buddies.

The two were spotted together last Thursday in Los Angeles at a star-studded party hosted by Paul's fashion designer daughter Stella McCartney.

The event was in honor of Stella's 18-year partnership with Adidas, according to a release, and featured a DJ, live performers and an 'immersive roller-skating piece by L.A Roller Girls'.

Onlookers say Paul (80) and Ringo (82) chatted animatedly for most of the night, even taking time to bust some moves at the edge of the dance floor.

'They were thick as thieves' says one attendee. 'I was standing like, about ten feet away from them for the whole thing, it was amazing. Then - Paul seemed to notice something, and sat up straight. He nudged Ringo and was pointing at one of the roller skaters. Like he recognised something. She had a jumpsuit on with a pattern, little red horses on black.

'Paul gave Stella a hug and just found it so funny. He rushed over to Ringo and was pointing at it.

'Whatever it was Ringo suddenly burst out laughing too. Absolute fits. The pair of them could barely stand by the end.

97

'I was talking to Stella afterwards – she's known Ringo since she was a child, of course. She said she's literally never seen him looking happier.'

[98]

BEATLE WINDFALL FOR LOCAL CHARITY

A LOCAL cat charity got the cream earlier this week thanks to a mysterious donation...

Staff at the Cats' Protection League shop in Henley are well-used to donations of clothes or toys being left on their doorstep, but one box last Tuesday was rather different.

Shop manager Mark Stapleton of Rosehill said: 'It caught my eye at once. The top was open and you could see it was full of Beatles albums – all in immaculate condition; the one where they're a brass band, the one with no cover, that one where they're a drawing. Looked like a full set.'

'Sara at the bakery's a Beatles fan and told me the records in the box are all 'first pressings'' he explained. 'And the first five or six are all 'stereo'; Sara said this makes them much rarer. The one with them leaning over a balcony's got a black and gold label, which she seemed pretty excited about.'

Armed with this knowledge Mark got in touch with local auction house Tappins, who will be putting the collection under the hammer on 28th July. The reserve price for the ten records is £10,000 with a possible final sale price of several times that. All proceeds will go to the Cats' Protection League.

98

Asked if there was anything else in the box Mark said: 'Just an envelope with a faded note in reading 'To George. A gift. Seeing as you liked it so much. GM' pinned to an old-fashioned silk tie with a sort of horse pattern.

'I binned the letter and put the tie straight on the racks for 75p. It's still there. If I'm honest I wouldn't buy it either.'

Henley Standard **June 16 1995**

[99]

GEORGE HARRISON: Everything was kind of falling apart. I went to Haight-Ashbury thinking it was going to be this groovy place with little shops and hippy people making works of art. But many of them turned out to be... bums. Very young kids who'd dropped acid and gone to this mecca of LSD. I was really afraid because I could see all these spotty youths and still this undercurrent of Beatlemania but from a... twisted angle.

It showed me what was happening in the drug culture, it wasn't all these groovy people having spiritual awakenings and being artistic. It was like any addiction.

So I took LSD one last time. The dreaded Lysergic. I had some in a little bottle and I put some under a microscope while I was high and it was like... a bit of old rope.

Then I realised, it wasn't old rope. I could see the little red pattern on black. It was a tie. It was THE tie.

I saw us back there in Studio Two's control room – and realised it was kind of the start. The sun was coming up and I just sat there, thinking about that moment, seeing all these various different ways it could have happened.

Strange that it came to me at that moment - when it was all getting too complicated. *A tie.* The ties between us, the ties we made for people. They'll last. '*It is not dying*' as the song says.

99

Then a Scottish hybrid of John and Paul offered me Ringo's suitcase from Rishikesh and I went to bed.'

The Beatles Anthology, **Episode Seven**

[100]

GEORGE HARRISON: [ctd] always expanding. You know? It's something we should all take very seriously, because if we don't...[LAUGHS] it'll be the end of us.

SAMIRA AHMED: Looking back over the past twenty years what are you most proud of?

GEORGE HARRISON: If you're talking about something which did some good in the world it's probably the Handmade Foundation's work in India – you know, it takes so little, comparatively I mean. Clean water. You pay for a few classrooms. It's relatively straightforward.

SAMIRA AHMED: You surprised everyone during the early stages of the pandemic...

GEORGE HARRISON: The Zoom thing? That was enjoyable to be fair. Getting the three of us together to bring a bit of ...'fabness' to the world [LAUGHS]...

SAMIRA AHMED: How did you decide which songs to do?

GEORGE HARRISON: For me, it was the ones I could remember. Which was none of them. [LAUGHS]. Opening with 'Misery' was Paul's idea, I remember. Ringo was dead keen to do Yellow Submarine for all the cooped-up kiddies. All My Loving went better than I thought it would... I was glad we got to do The Inner Light – that's a song with a real message I think. And I've always wanted to do Every Little Thing live, as that's one we never got to do when we were together.

SAMIRA AHMED: And ending on All Together Now just felt very...right. That gig...those thirty minutes meant so much to people around the world.

GEORGE HARRISON: If there's any point to this ...thing the four of us had, that's it surely? Cheering people up.

SAMIRA AHMED: So Sir George Harrison, you've reached the milestone of eighty. So many Beatle moments have become iconic. They get reinterpreted again and again. Is there any one incident that somehow... sticks in your mind? Perhaps from the early days? Something that summed up that phenomenal confidence The Beatles had?

GEORGE HARRISON: No. Not really.

APPENDICES

(1)

With the session over, it was time for the thumb-sized group to make the long trip back up to Liverpool. Due to its size, the group's 1:25 scale Commer van could only travel at 12 mph so it took tiny, gaunt Neil Aspinall three days to drive the musicians and their little instruments back up to Liverpool. The band arrived back in town just in time for their homecoming show in the Cavern, abseiling down each of the club's twenty eight steps using bound-together banana skins from the fruit warehouse over the road. This 9th June show became notorious among Cavernites, due to another of John Lennon's shocking on-stage pranks. 'At first when he came on we couldn't see what was different' said Lindy Ness. 'But some of us in the front row, the real obsessives, used to bring magnifying glasses to all the shows, so we could see what they were doing. I had a particularly strong magnifying glass, borrowed from my dad who was a detective with Merseyside Police, so I was the first to notice – John had come on with a toilet seat around his neck! He must have got it from a doll's house or something,' The session ended in near tragedy however, when Sue Cement Mixer's magnifying glass focused a beam from the snack bar's illuminated sign onto Paul's jacket, causing it to catch light.

Luckily quick-thinking Bob Wooler quenched the flames by tipping his cup of tea over the bass player. Afterwards an enraged Brian Epstein invoiced Wooler 1s 1/2d for dry cleaning of the tiny suit.

Tune In, **Mark Lewisohn 2010**

(2)

BEATLES ANNOUNCE FINAL RECORD

London, 2023

The Beatles are soon to release their final new song, according to Paul McCartney.

Speculation about the release began when Paul McCartney let slip in an interview to promote his new photography exhibition that he and fellow surviving Beatle Ringo Starr had been working on an uncompleted song by one of their deceased bandmates.

'It was about six months ago that I got the call' said Paul 'Olivia said she'd been cataloguing George's tape reels and found a cassette with 'For Ringo (and Paul)' on the label.

'I was stunned, as you can imagine. Olivia had the tape digitised and sent over the file and straight away I recognised the song. It was 'I Don't Like Your Tie', which must have been one of the first songs George ever wrote.

I think he even wanted us to do it for our first Parlophone session but me and John, being the Big I Am in those days, weren't having it.

'So Ringo and I both had a listen and y'know... reacquainted ourselves with this song and...it's a great little number. It didn't take us long to agree to finish it off.'

McCartney was quick to clarify rumours about AI's role in the new recording.

'I've heard a lot of speculation about so-called AI' he said 'and we want to be completely above-board with everyone: yes, we've used AI. We've used a tonne of it. How else were we going to get John on there? We fed it must have been 150 hours of recordings of John into the programme and it got a pretty good handle on his voice, so every second you hear of John on this new one is AI.

'We've also used AI to replace the voice and guitar on George's demo, plus my and Ringo's parts are AI too. The whole thing sounds great.

'And just wait 'til you see the video.'

REDDIT GROUP: F@bFour:TieMen. Thread 356 11.32 9th July 2021.

FELPINMANSIONS32: Anyone heard the new BeatleFabCast yet (ep 355)? Great interview with none other than Ted Marshall – as discovered by this very subreddit!!

RINGOFAN92: Way to go Ted! :)

JOSH346: BeatleFabCast is a bust. 'America's #1 Beatles Podcast' my ASS!

FELPINMANSIONS32: Great to see Ted getting some recognition for his role in our guys' story eh @JOSH346

JOSH346: Why do you say that?

FELPINMANSIONS32: @JOSH346 You FOUND him dude, and now he's like in the limelight – RESULT!

JOSH346: Ted Marshall's a fake and a phony and you can TELL HIM I SAID THAT.

RINGOFAN92: :(So he didn't fit the hinge on Studio Two's control room door? He WASN'T there???

JOSH346: He was there fwiw but like I said after I met him, dude doesn't remember SHIT. But ever since he spoke to me he's all 'The lads' this and 'The lads' that.

ALLANKLEINSHUSBAND: A little bird tells me he has a book in the works too!

JOSH346: Saying WHAT? He couldn't remember a SINGLE

THING when I spoke to him and now he's carrying on like he's Ron freakin' Richards.

MARTHASCOLLAR: Just listened :) So great to hear all his memories!

JOSH346: HE DOESN'T REMEMBER ANYTHING!!!

MARTHASCOLLAR: He talks a lot about Norman sending Chris Neal down to the canteen.

JOSH346: BECAUSE I **TOLD** HIM >:(>:(>:(

RINGOFAN92: Eggpod just tweeted that Ted's their next guest. He's going to be talking about Gone Troppo!!

JOSH346: HE THOUGHT ONE OF THEM WAS CALLED STEPHEN!!!!

ALLANKLEINSHUSBAND: Pre-orders are open on amazon for his book btw. Pub date 31st May 2025.

JOSH346 HAS LEFT THE CHAT

RINGOFAN92: If you had to cut the White Album down to one disc, what would you leave off?

JOSH364 HAS ENTERED THE CHAT

JOSH346: I'm not having this. Going to prove he's full of it. 100 upvotes to the first person who can get me Chris Neal's email address...

(4)

In a land tangled with the vines of speech, a great king asked four warriors if anything troubled their hearts. The youngest of them replied: 'Your tie'.

The great king wept, and the beast within the warriors, ambition, drove them weeping on to the jagged rocks of pride.

Translation of cuneiform tablet, c.2100 BCE Mesopotamia

(5)

MECHA-RINGO OPERATIONAL LOG 4 // GG +++ PEACE
AND LOVE++ FAULT REPORT TRANSMISSION INCOMING
++++++ ZRXXQ3 /12/43338 MECHA-RINGO UNIT CELL C5
COMPROMISED +++++ ACTION IN TRANSIT +++ VIA TRASMAT
INSTANCE 4 F 4 FF CELL BREACHED ERROR 555 REQ ACTION
44 ACTION ++++ ENGAGED ENEMY – LOCATION: LIBERTYS
TIE DEPT. HOSTILE ACTION SEQUENCE INTITIATED. HOSTILE
ACTION SEQUENCE ABORTED D/TO APPEARANCE OF JOHN
LENNON FROM ANTIVERSE +++ GEORGE HARRISON IN TIE
RACK NEUTRALISED BY JOHN LENNON FROM ANTIVERSE +++
MECHA-RINGO UNIT SURPLUS TO REQMENTS +++ MECHA-
RINGO UNIT INITIATED STANDARD PROCEDURE 14: AUTO-
PORT TO NEXT TACTICAL NEXUS +++ PEACE AND LOVE
+++ DESTINATION ERROR 04/04/1968BCE TARGET ERROR
MISIDENTIFICATION MALFUNCTION PETERANDGORDON
ELIMINATED IN ERROR. TELEGRAM/FLOWERS PROTOCOL
TO FAMILIES OF PETERANDGORDON INITIATED. OIL LEVEL
CHECK COMPLETE +++ OIL LEVEL WITHIN OPERATIONAL
PARAMETERS. BATTERY LOW +++ PEACE AND LOVE +++
MECHA-RINGO UNIT TO RETURN TO DINGLE FOR BATTERY
RE-CHARGE AND COUNTRY AND WESTERN RECORDS. MECHA-
RINGO TO TRANSMAT IN SEVEN SECONDS +++ MECHA-RINGO
INCOMING +++ PEACE AND LOVE +++

(6)

Britain under the Nazis: 1941 to 1967.

'FORGOTTEN VOICES OF THE OCCUPATION' Imperial War Museum. Audio file 1466/b rec May 4, 1989.

PRISCILLA WHITE:

By the time I worked the cloakroom they'd renamed it the Hohle Club. What people forget about the Nazis is all the admin, endless chits of paper, y'know? There were thousands of them typing away in the Royal Liver, as we still called it. But admin means typists and I tell you, those Nazi girls *loved* the boys. The lads spent most of their time doing these... sudden gigs, all hush- hush, sneaking off for when they could. But the day job was still turning up to play bloody German folk music and 'Falling In Love Again' for the typists. As it was Liverpool there were a few Nazi big names there, y'know, overseeing the port. They'd sit at the back smoking, the Nazi girls would be sat in rows just bursting with excitement at these handsome lads. You could see them wanting to get up and dance but after each one they'd do these quick little claps, all smiling.

Now and again there'd be a bomb, or a raid, the bigwigs would rush off, probably didn't want to be buried in the Hohle. So they'd all head out and the girls would leg it back to their offices.

Stupid, the Hohle was probably the safest place in Liverpool.

The streets were deserted. That's when they'd come in. All the locals, my mates, the shoppers, little kids. John would peer over and say '*We all right 'Cill?*' and I'd give the thumbs up. And then... dickie bows off, they'd mess up their hair, then they'd really play, all the girls screaming. It was great.

They had one... She Loves You. Can't remember how it went, but it was about someone you know bursting in with good news. Back then? Imagine that.

(7)

ALBERTO SUMAC: It must have been February '62 when the Englishman came. In an Andes hill town any new face gets noticed straightaway. At first he stayed in the guesthouse, then after a while he bought that tall house on at the end of the main street. People said they'd seen crates arriving from Lima; he had an electrician come and put in a mains supply. Three weeks later a sign went up: 'Recording Studio'. Me and my friends had been playing music together since we were kids – village dances, feast days. We were there the day after he put up the sign. He said his name was Señor Martin. We played him some of our songs, just guitars, maracas and an old packing case as a drum. He said we were rough but we had something and he'd like to put us on tape. We asked why he'd come to our little town; he said he'd worked in a studio in England but could never find the kind of act he was looking for. He said he felt he might have found it in us. He asked if there was anything we didn't like so Jorge said 'Well for starters I don't like your neckerchief.' Señor Martin burst out laughing and we all joined in. From then on we were in there almost every night. Our first tape came out so well that Señor Martin had 100 copies pressed up at the plant in Huancayo and sold them in markets all around the area. The second record sold 300 copies, the third 500. Señor Martin was wonderful to work with – so supportive but also always pushing us to do our best. I remember once he'd been in town for about a year he was joined by an English woman; Judy. They were married in the church on the hill. As the years went on we kept making music with Señor Martin and became famous in the region. Through the end of the sixties, the seventies and eighties it went on – people bought our records and came to our concerts but no one bothered us or wanted anything of us but music. We've slowed down a little in recent years – it's 2024 and we're all in our eighties – Señor Martin doesn't talk about his age but he must be more than ninety. We're due back in the studio with him tomorrow in fact – he's got some ideas for manipulating samples to go over Paolo's new tune – it's really exciting. We could never have dreamed this life, and I'm glad Señor Martin found what he was looking for.

INDEX

Alex, Magic: traumatises George Martin with innovative tie, 120

Anhalt-Köthen, Leopold, Prince of: 114

Beatles, The: misplace harmonica, 44; ask pertinent questions, 17; sit meekly like schoolboys, 27; disinclination to play George Harrison song about ties, 40; very tiny stature of, 108; acorn collecting career of, 118; near-nakedness of, 2; seasickness suffered by,151; have gig disrupted by the Gestapo, 155

Best, Pete: has good idea, 34; sits motionless for 15 hours,70

Bowles, Peter: 61

Chalomet, Timothée: discussion of aesthetic qualities, 132

Drake, Charlie: 54

Epstein, Brian: bisection by The Amazing Alexandro, 110; inability to spell 'Parlophone', 7

Fascher, Horst: considers punching George Martin, 22

Printed in Great Britain
by Amazon